Middle-Power Korea
Contributions to the Global Agenda

COUNCIL *on*
FOREIGN
RELATIONS

Middle-Power Korea
Contributions to the Global Agenda

Colin I. Bradford, Toby Dalton,
Brendan Howe, Jill Kosch O'Donnell,
Andrew O'Neil, and Scott A. Snyder

Contents

Acknowledgments

This project was initiated as a result of a series of conversations I had with South Korean colleagues who observed that South Korea's thinking about the world had matured as a consequence of its own democratic development. South Koreans, long focused on the ongoing contest for legitimacy between South and North Korea and South Korea's own experience with modernization, had developed both the capability and the willingness to look beyond the peninsula with a view toward marking South Korea's place in and contributions to the world. As a result, South Koreans were able to make their own contributions to international leadership, both as a way of paying the world back for decades of international support and as a way of sharing with the world its unique experiences with development and democratization. Between 2010 and 2013, South Korea made a concerted effort to host a series of important multilateral forums, marking a new chapter in South Korea's experience as a convener and contributor to the international agenda. This short volume evaluates the sustainability of those initial contributions and their significance for South Korea's global role.

The CFR program on U.S.-Korea policy extends its thanks to the Korea Foundation, including President Yu Hyun-seok, former President Kim Woosang, Director of Policy and Research Kim Tae-hwan, and Washington Branch Director Si-yeon Lee, as well as the Smith Richardson Foundation for their support for the project. Additional programmatic support from the Korea International Trade Association has enabled the production and distribution of this volume.

I greatly appreciate the assistance of the Asan Institute for Policy Studies, especially President Hahm Chaibong and Senior Research Fellow Mo Jongryn, for hosting a valuable workshop held in January 2015 in Seoul, at which the chapter authors benefited from the critical review of their initial drafts by Korean experts.

Special thanks are due to the chapters' authors: Colin I. Bradford, Toby Dalton, Brendan Howe, Jill Kosch O'Donnell, and Andrew O'Neil, all of whom provided keen insight into the specific areas of Korea's contributions based on their specific issue expertise. They have been diligent and gracious throughout the workshop discussion and review process. I also appreciate the input of our Korean colleagues who served as discussants for our contributors: Lee Tae-joo, Kang Seonjou, Choi Hyeonjung, Park Siwon, Shin Chang-Hoon, Nam Chang-hee, Song In-chang, and Yoon Deok-ryong. Their insights helped ground—and in some cases, reorient—the chapters in this volume.

I would like to thank Senior Vice President and Director of Studies James M. Lindsay for his support and valuable comments that strengthened the final product. CFR Publications staff Patricia Dorff and Ashley Bregman ably, patiently, and efficiently edited and managed the production of the publication. Amy Baker in the Studies Program was helpful in her support and advice for the project. I also appreciate the support of Tricia Miller Klapheke and Jake Meth in the Global Communications and Media Relations department. Finally, I would like to thank Research Associate Darcie Draudt for managing the project and publication process.

Scott A. Snyder
June 2015

Acronyms

APEC	Asia-Pacific Economic Cooperation
ASEAN	Association of Southeast Asian Nations
DAC	Development Assistance Committee
DEEP	Development Experience Exchange Program
DPRK	Democratic People's Republic of Korea
CIDC	Committee for International Development Cooperation
CPI	Climate Policy Initiative
EDCF	Economic Development Cooperation Fund
ETS	emissions trading scheme
FDI	foreign direct investment
GCF	Green Climate Fund
GDP	gross domestic product
GGGI	Global Green Growth Initiative
GNI	gross national income
G20	Group of Twenty
IAEA	International Atomic Energy Association
IMF	International Monetary Fund
INDC	intended nationally distributed contributions
IPCC	Intergovernmental Panel on Climate Change
KAERI	Korea Atomic Energy Research Institute
KDI	Korea Development Institute
KEPCO	Korea Electric Power Company
KF	Korea Fund
KOICA	Korea Overseas International Cooperation Agency

KSP	Knowledge Sharing Program
MDG	Millennium Development Goal
MIKTA	Mexico, Indonesia, South Korea, Turkey, and Australia
MOFAT	Ministry of Foreign Affairs and Trade
MOSF	Ministry of Strategy and Finance
NDA	national designated authority
NGO	nongovernmental organization
NSG	Nuclear Suppliers Group
NSS	Nuclear Security Summit
ODA	official development assistance
OECD	Organization for Economic Cooperation and Development
PCSD	Presidential Committee for Sustainable Development
PSAG	private-sector advisory group
PSF	private-sector facility
ROK	Republic of Korea
SDG	Sustainable Development Goal
UN	United Nations
UNDP	United Nations Development Program
UNFCCC	United Nations Framework Convention on Climate Change
USAID	United States Agency for International Development

Introduction

The successful development and democratization of the Republic of Korea (ROK), or South Korea, have enabled the country to rise to the top of many indices of economic and political success that no one would have dreamed possible in the aftermath of the Korean War, or even in the 1970s and 1980s, when the building blocks of the country's modernization were in place but under the direction of a repressive military dictatorship. In the 1990s, the Asian financial crisis raised vociferous domestic criticisms that then President Kim Young-sam had prematurely rushed South Korea's 1996 entry into the Organization for Economic Cooperation and Development (OECD) without sufficient preparation, even as the ROK's largest companies continued to extend their global reach in a wide range of sectors and markets. By the 2000s, developing countries increasingly looked to South Korea as a potential model of modernization and democratization, but not necessarily as a global leader. It was clear from the faces of President Lee Myung-bak and his top leadership upon their return to Seoul from the Group of 20 (G20) summit in Pittsburgh in the fall of 2009 that, having landed Seoul hosting rights to the third G20 summit meeting for the following year, they considered their trip a great victory—one that would open new frontiers for South Korean diplomacy on the international stage.

But despite hosting the summit, it was not at all clear what to expect from South Korea's performance in the run-up to the 2010 G20. Nor was it clear whether the ROK, as a middle power, would be able to muster substantial influence or easily manage potential clashes between the great powers as the lead caretaker and broker of the global agenda. It seemed a formidable task for South Korea as a relative newcomer to the international scene to be able to make a distinctly Korean leadership contribution to the G20 summit. For South Koreans, the success of their country as host of these major gatherings has raised the question of how it, as a successful economic modernizer that is not a major power, can make its mark on the international political agenda. To respond to this question, South Korean opinion leaders have increasingly investigated the idea of the ROK as a middle power as a primary framework for evaluating the opportunities and constraints arising from its emerging international role. The attraction of this concept, at least in its initial stage, has been affirmed by South Korea's subsequent role and interest in the establishment of a like-minded grouping of select G20 participants called MIKTA (for Mexico, Indonesia, South Korea, Turkey, and Australia).

The essays commissioned in this volume provide an initial evaluation of South Korean efforts to make substantive contributions to the international agenda as a middle power through the "hosting diplomacy" the country conducted between 2010 and 2012: the G20 summit; the OECD Development Assistance Committee (DAC) meeting; the Nuclear Security Summit; and the Green Climate Fund. Each of the following chapters assesses from a functional perspective the ROK's contributions to these international forums, both as a host and as an ongoing leader in each of the areas where hosting has provided the opportunity to play an ongoing role.

The chapters' authors—Colin Bradford on South Korea's leadership on financial policy, Brendan Howe on its contributions to international development, Toby Dalton on its contributions to the nuclear sector, and Jill Kosch O'Donnell on its green growth leadership—explain the ROK's preparations and efforts and the follow-up activities that emanated from its hosting roles. Now that some time has passed, this project can assess the ongoing impact of South Korea's contributions and its potential to make a difference in these areas. The assessments conclude with an insightful peer-review evaluation by Andrew O'Neil, who offers a perspective from Australia—a country that has also reflected on its middle-power role—on the ROK's actual and potential contributions to middle-power diplomacy.

Collectively, this volume serves as an after-action report assessing South Korea's hosting diplomacy by providing an assessment of its short-term effects on and potential lasting offerings to each of the areas covered. The authors assess the effectiveness of South Korean efforts, offering some insight into how the country can set realistic goals and recognize the reasonable limits of the convening role on the international stage. They also offer insight into the factors necessary for middle powers to consider as they seek to maximize their impact in niche areas despite their limited size and diplomatic resources.

It is clear that the ROK's hosting diplomacy has raised the country's international profile and standing. This is represented unscientifically by the fact that, during his first six years as president, Barack Obama has visited South Korea more than any country other than Mexico. Moreover, South Korea's hosting of high-profile summits has changed its population's perception of its own country as a leader on the international stage. Finally, the ROK has proven itself able to contribute in the areas for which it has played a hosting role.

This collection makes a number of important observations and recommendations for South Korea's future role as a convener and contributor to international diplomatic forums. The harder questions for the country center on three areas: the sustainability of its contributions, both in terms of institutional persistence and its political will to sustain particular issues as a component of a long-term international brand; the transferability of South Korea's experience, and the applicability of that experience to other cases; and the effectiveness of the instruments available to the country as a middle power for substantively influencing the international and regional agendas.

CHALLENGES TO SOUTH KOREA'S MIDDLE-POWER STRATEGY

The sustainability of South Korea's efforts to influence the diplomatic agenda is particularly pertinent given the limited role it is able to play as a non–great power seeking to influence the direction of international affairs. Given its limited technical, diplomatic, and human resources, South Korea's ability to prioritize international contributions will be essential for avoiding being spread too thin. Initially, the ROK attempted to link the themes of development, energy, and green growth with distinct approaches that appeared to provide it with an "ideas advantage." By bringing a new idea to the table or providing thought leadership to add something valuable to the discussion, rather than simply relying on the size of its stake in a particular issue, South Korea was able to justify a voice disproportionate to its relative contribution of physical resources. However, there is a risk that hosting for the sake of hosting on a wide range of functional issues could dilute the ROK's capacity to make effective niche additions to a clearly defined area that requires thought leadership. In his chapter in this volume, Andrew O'Neil points to the risk of "middle-power overstretch," a phenomenon in which countries such as South Korea could try to make contributions to international problems without "the capacity to make a difference toward resolving" the issue at hand.

Another aspect of sustainability under consideration here is the need for lasting institutional commitment to dedicate resources and human capital so that the contribution of South Korean ideas may be sustained well past the diplomatic event for which they were originally mobilized. As Colin Bradford, Brendan Howe, and Toby Dalton point out in their respective chapters, the ROK has mobilized its bureaucracy effectively in support of hosting multilateral meetings, but following the meetings themselves, the human resource base dedicated to preparing for the leader-level event has dispersed. There has not been a mechanism through which to leverage the aggregate experience gained through hosting several of these events. Without such a mechanism to sustain deepening expertise on specific issues such as global financial policy and nuclear security, South Korea also loses an opportunity to sustain its intellectual offerings in these areas.

In addition, the sustainability of South Korean contributions in the issue areas under study has been damaged by the familiar difficulty of maintaining the attention paid to particular issues from administration to administration. The current Park Geun-hye administration has tended to downplay any issues where "successes" might be associated with the legacy and efforts of the preceding administration of Lee Myung-bak. As a result, the main emphases of prior administrations are destined to gather cobwebs when new political leadership comes into power. Yet some of these areas, such as international development and clean energy, also represent areas where the ROK is institutionally poised to continue to make a difference—for example, President Park co-chaired the thematic session on climate finance at the September 2014 United Nations (UN) Climate Summit. Instances such as these can enable presidents to supersede the efforts of their predecessors if they have the acumen and political will to do so.

A second factor that has proven to be a challenge for South Korean leadership on international development is the transferability of the ROK's own experience to other countries. In other words, is the South Korean development experience sui generis, or can it provide lessons for other developing countries? As Brendan Howe points out, South Korea's robust commitment to sharing experience through its Knowledge Sharing Program (KSP) and its capacity to host specialists from other countries for technical training has served as a powerful vehicle by which it can make positive contributions to international develop-ment. But the wholesale transfer of programs on the model of the ROK's *saemaul*, or "new village," development program has yielded caution-ary statements against a cookie-cutter approach as well as criticisms that the program prioritizes growth at the expense of human develop-ment. Toby Dalton similarly notes that the Korea Institute for Nuclear Accounting and Control is involved in international training on safe-guards and nuclear safety culture that, to be effective, should replace existing cultural norms in the new host country with internationally accepted nonproliferation safeguard standards.

A third issue raised in this collection is related to the effectiveness of the instruments available to the ROK as a middle power to influence the international agenda. This effectiveness of South Korean efforts should be evaluated on multiple levels, including their size and scope, relative impact, and context. The size-and-scope constraints are particularly relevant to other middle powers that have finite resources to bring as levers for influence in dealing with international challenges. These con-straints are evident in the small share of South Korean development assistance as a component of global finances available for development purposes and in the limited influence of South Korean pledges to cut emissions compared with those of larger (and richer) greenhouse gas emitters. Yet contributions to a growth-centered model for evaluating development effectiveness versus aid effectiveness, the prioritization of green growth as a potentially useful adaptation strategy for combating the effects of climate change, and efforts to play a bridging role between developing and developed countries in global finance discussions all represent intangible thought leadership disproportionate to the ROK's relative stake or size.

Another dimension of South Korean effectiveness as a middle power has centered on soft-power instruments as tools of influence. Colin Bradford argues that the ROK has effectively deployed middle-power strengths—including vision, institutions, and skilled individuals—to make an effective contribution to the international agenda. Brendan Howe takes a more cautious view on the effectiveness of soft power, noting that a focus on its assets can lead to a seemingly inherent empha-sis on branding and overselling of contributions to all nations.

Finally, the perceived effectiveness of South Korea's role as a middle power depends on context. On the one hand, the ROK has progressively moved from outlier to connecting node as the intensity of its efforts in a variety of areas such as finance, international development, and green growth has increased. By leveraging its role as connector, the country has placed itself closer to the center in addressing specific issues through the power of networks. This approach has been particularly effective in raising South Korea's international profile on global issues.

On the other hand, in a regional context, South Korea remains constrained by its focus on the surrounding great powers, in particular the United States and China. This geographical context has meant mixed benefits for the ROK: on global finance, it has arguably benefited from its proximity to China at a time when financial power is flowing to Asia but China's influence in international financial forums is not yet fully formed. At the Busan meeting of the OECD DAC in 2011, South Korea brokered an inclusive dialogue that bridged the gap between emerging and established donors for the first time. The country's green growth impact was disproportionate to its size, but still insignificant when compared with U.S.-China bilateral targets announced on the sidelines of the 2014 Asia-Pacific Economic Cooperation (APEC) meeting in Beijing. Despite South Korea's regional bridging efforts, as represented by its fledgling Northeast Asia Peace and Cooperation Initiative, its viability as a middle power on the international stage remains easier to grasp than it is in a Northeast Asian context.

RECOMMENDATIONS FOR SOUTH KOREA

Taken together, the following chapters suggest that South Korea carry out these steps in its efforts to adopt a greater international leadership role:

- *Avoid "middle-power overstretch" by prioritizing commitments in line with both a clearly recognizable brand and deep niche expertise on specific global issues.* For instance, the ROK has already made a mark by identifying cross-cutting issues that play to its comparative advantage vis-à-vis requisite technology or human resources, such as sustainable development, energy efficiency, and climate and development finance. In this respect, the ROK should be well positioned to build on its past contributions to these areas in the Post-2015 Development Agenda and Sustainable Development Goals (SDG) for 2030 as well as at the December 2015 UN Climate Change Conference in Paris.

- *Establish institutional and human-resource development strategies for sustaining follow-up contributions in designated priority areas in order to have a lasting influence on the issue areas concerned.* In this way, South Korea may ensure a lasting contribution to the world as a follow-up to its meeting diplomacy. The country needs to consider an institutional-bureaucratic strategy for revisiting and maintaining its contributions on designated issues so they are recognized as areas of strength and as calling cards for the ROK's diplomatic brand on the international stage. These bureaucratic-support mechanisms should make it easier to sustain political will across administrations for a particular set of priorities even when administrations change.

- *Carefully assess and regularly reassess development experience to determine which factors are most transferable to the context of specific developing countries.* South Korea should simultaneously take advantage of its strong human-resource base to provide technical training and assistance in aspects of development for which it has a particularly strong record.

By exploiting its international standing, capabilities, and aspirations as a middle power, South Korea has drawn a record number of leaders to Seoul for discussions on some of the toughest problems facing the world and has earned a seat at the table based on its thought leadership rather than its size. But for a country with limited resources and power such as the ROK to continue to make a difference on the international stage, it needs to effectively deploy its vision and experience, its institutional capacity to bridge gaps among nations, and its top-rank human resources. To achieve this goal and avoid "middle-power overstretch," South Korea should take the necessary steps to ensure that it prioritizes its efforts and ensures that those efforts are sustainable, transferable, and effective.

South Korea as a Middle Power in Global Governance: "Punching Above Its Weight" Based on National Assets and Dynamic Trajectory

Colin I. Bradford

In early December 2014, on the Air France bus route into Paris from Charles de Gaulle Airport, several neon-lit advertisements dotted the landscape against the dark sky. Among them, ads for LG, Hyundai, Samsung, and KIA stood out, symbolic of South Korea's visible presence in continental Europe. One had to be impressed by how this country of now 50 million people has become a significant global economic power over the past sixty years, rising from the shattering experience of the Korean War as a poor developing country. It is a historical trajectory of dynamic development, unmatched by any other nation; it gives South Korea a narrative and a trajectory that continuously reinvigorates its dynamism.

Today, as a result of its economic vigor, South Korea has achieved the status of a "middle power" in global relations and is a significant contributor to global governance. It is not only a member of the G20 summit group of the world's largest economies, but also a leader in it, having hosted, in Seoul in 2010, the G20 summit—the first emerging nation to do so—and it has continuously pushed for reform and strengthening of the global system of international institutions.

Questions about the ROK's future include: What are the foundations of South Korea's middle power status? How has it exerted global influence? And what are the challenges and prospects for South Korea's continuing role as a constructive contributor to global governance?

THE GLOBAL CONTEXT FOR MIDDLE POWERS

Middle powers play an important role in moving the world toward greater international cooperation and in shifting the focus of international relations toward the common good. Today's global system, whereby economic and military power is concentrated in only a few nations, necessitates middle powers to balance the international agenda. In a world of growing complexity, diversity, and interconnectedness, in which interests and ideals seek visibility and voice, there is a new imperative to find mechanisms, modalities, and means by which a variety of viewpoints come to bear on issues that influence global decisions and outcomes. To compensate for their size and relative lack of military strength, middle powers need to rely on soft-power skills (knowledge, expertise, organization, preparation, discipline, leadership, and institutions) to represent the social, environmental, and human interests of humanity.

There are sixteen middle powers that have seats at the G20. The four "great powers" are the United States, China, Russia, and the European Union. The strength of the G20 is that it embeds the great powers in a body in which middle powers with weight, clout, and influence constitute the majority of the other members. When the discussion of Syria came up at the G20 summit in St. Petersburg in 2013, and Ukraine became a major issue in Brisbane in 2014, tensions and conflicts consequential to the entire world were thrashed out by the great powers within the context of a plurality of middle powers. Hence, for middle

TABLE 1: GREAT POWERS AND MIDDLE POWERS

G20 Great Powers	G20 Middle Powers		Middle Powers Outside the G20	
China	ASIA	Australia	EUROPE	Spain
European Union		India	The Nordics	Denmark
Russia		Indonesia		Finland
United States		Japan		Norway
		South Korea		Sweden
	EUROPE	France	OTHER	Chile
		Germany		Iran
		Italy		Israel
		United Kingdom		Nigeria
				Singapore
	LATIN AMERICA	Argentina		Spain
		Brazil		
		Mexico		
	NORTH AMERICA	Canada		
	OTHER	Saudi Arabia		
		South Africa		
		Turkey		

powers, the G20 is a major forum for the exercise of their roles and influence. But it is, of course, not the only venue for doing so.

For South Korea to contribute to the global agenda and strengthen its role as a global leader, it should continue to build on its assets as a middle power. The historical narrative of South Korea's economic transformation is a major source of national strength. The ongoing drama of the ROK's evolving national narrative keeps feeding back into the narrative itself, intensifying South Korea's forward momentum.[1] The leadership of exceptional individuals at crucial moments continues to be important for South Korea's middle-power diplomacy and global leadership. The institutional innovation of using presidential committees as a means of managing cross-sectoral, cross-ministerial, private-public sector challenges sets a twenty-first-century standard for addressing global challenges that now require comprehensive integrated approaches beyond the specialized, silo-driven methods of the previous century. This governance innovation could be extremely relevant to countries as they turn to implement the Post–2015 Development Agenda and the Sustainable Development Goals for 2030. The role of major South Korean institutions in generating a "deep bench" of international leaders is essential for the future.

The role of middle powers in global leadership in the coming years may depend more than previously believed on the ability of South Korea to lead other middle powers in grasping their role and importance in the global system of international institutions. But South Korea cannot play the middle-power role alone. Only if others begin to follow the ROK's lead in being proactive, intentional, strategic, and ambitious will other nations benefit fully from the potential contributions of middle powers.

South Korea's leadership role in the loose coalition of middle powers known as MIKTA—Mexico, Indonesia, South Korea, Turkey, and Australia—is an example of pulling together a group of promising middle powers to anticipate issues within the G20 summit preparations and other forums. Nonetheless, it is probably more beneficial if middle-power coalitions remain fluid—capable of shifting concerted actions among differing clusters of countries—rather than try to force consensus on all issues among the same group of countries.

"Shifting coalitions of consensus" generate benefits for middle powers and for the larger context as well.[2] Furthermore, and perhaps most important, bloc formation within the G20 or other forums would certainly not contribute to optimal global outcomes, since blocs would presume identical interests on a variety of issues based on fundamental strategic differences—when in fact those are the differences that need to be bridged and brokered. Allowing fluid middle-power coalitions means allowing patterns of power that can reconfigure themselves in response to evolving negotiations, facilitating their forward movement. Great-power relations can be leavened and lifted by adroit middle-power diplomacy, opening options not otherwise possible in face-offs lacking middle powers.

Hence, mechanisms such as the G20, in which middle powers are fully involved alongside great powers, provide major opportunities for the exercise of middle-power leadership and influence.

VISIONING THE FUTURE

In the 1990s, South Korea began to reexamine its future. This national conversation and reflection by the nation's elite helped bring about a transition from an insular country to an outward-looking nation.[3] The visioning process built on, but differed from, the national planning processes of previous decades—whereas those were primarily convened and driven by the government, the visioning process was led by civil society. But both processes showed a proclivity in South Korea toward strategic thinking and defining a sense of national purpose and direction. Despite a long international debate in the 1980s and beyond about the nature of the "East Asian miracles" of rapid economic development, it becomes clear in retrospect that the dynamic economic growth experience of South Korea was driven neither by a purely market-led, outward-oriented, trade-liberalizing model nor by a state-led, inward-looking, protectionist model. Rather, the exceptional economic performance of South Korea was and is derived from an interactive relationship between market and state, and between the public and private sectors, in which the dynamics that supported coexistence of the elements of the supposed dichotomies were more powerful than a choice of one would have been. Synergies and externalities were crucial; neither markets nor government alone would have been as successful in capturing them. In the end, the policy debates were of greater consequence for academics, theorists, and pundits than for the policymakers in both the private and public sectors in South Korea.

The ROK's success has been based more on growth-driven trade from the inside outward than by trade-driven growth from the outside inward.[4] What this interpretation highlights is the importance of internal sources of dynamism that drove economic performance over external forces inducing it: South Korea was responsible for its own destiny; its much-vaunted openness to the world economy was important, but it was not defining.

South Korea's role means that the narrative of national success is based more on internal dynamism resulting in rapidly increasing shares in global trade than on trade liberalization–induced, "getting prices right," export-led growth. The trajectory of South Korea is a story of "getting its act together" internally, creating synergies among sectors and institutions in a way that generated national dynamism that spilled over into an "export push." This narrative is an important source of energy for the ROK's future trajectory and roles because it highlights the degree to which the country used its national domestic assets and dynamics to generate a global thrust instead of relying on laissez-faire market forces and liberalization as neutral mechanisms for growth.

The South Korean success story is a story about intentionality, about the capacity of a society to define its future rather than to be passively lifted by market forces alone, and about the role of leadership, institutions, and narrative in determining destiny.

LEADERSHIP

Leadership, in the end, relies on whether there are individuals who have the right combination of substantive grasp, experience, credibility, and compelling personality to drive change and determine direction.

THE 2010 G20 SUMMIT IN SEOUL

When South Korea was chosen as chair of the fourth G20 summit, to take place in November 2010, President Lee Myung-bak made an innovation in organizing the team of officials who would prepare the summit. A presidential committee for the summit was formed under the leadership of Il SaKong, who served as finance minister in 1987–88. The sherpa (the most senior G20 advisor), Changyong Rhee, and the G20 finance deputy were in effect deputies to SaKong. In addition, the team of G20 officials, comprising representatives from the Ministry of Strategy and Finance, the Ministry of Foreign Affairs, the Bank of Korea, and the president's office—a total of 125 highly skilled, experienced, and dedicated senior officials and staff—were moved to a separate building near the Blue House (the official presidential residence) for the yearlong preparations. The building became the epicenter of South Korea's efforts to make its G20 summit a success. No other G20 country has chosen to organize its summit preparations in this way.

The principal priorities for South Korea in 2010 were getting agreements on macroeconomic imbalances, International Monetary Fund (IMF) reform, and a uniquely G20 thrust on development. The principals for the ROK on each of these issues were Rhee on macropolicy, Heenam Choi on IMF reform, and Wonhyuk Lim from the Korea Development Institute (KDI) on development. But there were other officials involved, both within the G20 team and in the respective government agencies and institutions. The strategic leader, catalyst, and orchestrator was SaKong, who had the seniority, stature, and political savvy to represent the presidential interest in the preparations. This novel arrangement served South Korea well, given that the Lee administration had high ambitions for achieving strong results.[5]

South Korea managed to get G20 agreement on a set of IMF reforms now known as the Seoul reforms, and on a set of nine priorities for global development cooperation now known as the Seoul development consensus. But despite heroic efforts by Rhee, the divergent views between the United States and China on macro imbalances and the inability of any leader to contain the discord over current account indicators led to a tremendous public debate in the period between the G20 finance ministers' meeting in Gyeongju in October 2010 and the G20 summit in Seoul the following month.

No amount of smoothing the diplomacy or wordsmithing the communiqué could hide the frictions and disagreements. In an unprecedented fashion, technical disagreements spilled into the global press for two full weeks, egged on by the world press without any mitigation by the summit leaders themselves. But no one has faulted the South Koreans for being ill-prepared or for not having held a significant summit. The divisions were too deep; leaders were not willing to bury differences for the sake of appearances. South Korea did not lose others' respect for presiding over a summit held in challenging circumstances.

A FINANCIAL COMMITMENT TO GREEN GROWTH

The ROK distinguished itself under President Lee by moving faster than most nations to embrace the realities of global climate change, to understand the dangers implicit in its own carbon-intensive high-growth path, and to adopt a comprehensive transformative strategy of green growth that would be more sustainable for South Korea's future.

The coincidence of Lee's election in 2007 and the celebration of the ROK's sixtieth anniversary on August 15, 2008, provided a window of opportunity to launch South Korea on the path toward green growth. In December 2007, president-elect Lee created a special committee on climate change. In February 2008, Lee established in the Blue House the National Future and Vision Office, and a year later he established the Presidential Committee on Green Growth. In April 2010, the cabinet approved and the president enacted the Framework Act on Low Carbon Green Growth, and in June 2010, Soogil Young was named the second head of the Presidential Committee on Green Growth, which oversaw the implementation of the Framework Act.[6]

The committee consisted of fifty members, one-third of whom were from the government, including six ministers; the other two-thirds were from the private sector. Young, who had been South Korean ambassador to the OECD, was an imaginative, innovative, and energetic leader with impressive intellectual depth and breadth. Under his leadership, green growth advanced from its conception as a national strategy to an action plan for the future. Furthermore, in 2010, the Global Green Growth Initiative (GGGI) was founded in Seoul; the first annual Global Green Growth Summit was held in June 2011. The first anniversary of the GGGI coincided with the fiftieth anniversary of the OECD and the fifteenth anniversary of South Korea's membership in the OECD.[7] Celebratory occasions helped advance a transformative national strategy of global consequence. And in 2012, South Korea worked with Mexico, the host of the 2012 G20 summit in Los Cabos, to bring green growth forward as a G20 priority and as a way of framing the global debate on systemic sustainability of energy and climate change.

This sequence of events and actions again demonstrates the importance of vision in shaping transformative strategies for South Korea's future; of presidential leadership in translating that vision into action; and of the use of a cross-ministerial, cross-sectoral presidential committee headed by dynamic, respected, and experienced leaders as the mechanism for implementing the nation's strategic vision.

A CONTINUING ROLE IN THE G20
AND A PROACTIVE PROFILE AT THE OECD

Even though South Korea is unlikely to chair the G20 summit again for many years, given the number of countries in the rotation, it has nonetheless maintained a high-profile role in G20 preparations and deliberations on the G20 summit process, on global economic policy issues, and on global economic governance.

One way to assert influence as a middle power is to play a proactive role in international settings, where command of substance and policy is more important than mastering diplomatic complexities and manners. The OECD is one such place; whereas the focus is on economic policy, many of the other issues—including energy, finance, trade, employment, environment, development, and science and technology—relate and interact with each other. Another way to realize greater influence as a middle power is to send teams of competent, experienced people to important international posts. For all the debate about "shares and chairs" at the IMF and efforts to redistribute quotas to align countries' voting power with their economic weight, in the end, who a government sends to sit in the chair is more important in terms of influence than the country's IMF voting share.

The South Korean ambassador to the OECD, Sihyung Lee, is a former ROK deputy trade minister. He has past experience with G20 summit matters from his post in the Ministry of Foreign Affairs and Trade, and he brought with him to the OECD a G20 hand, Ji-joon Kim, who has worked in both Washington and Seoul. Together, Ambassador Lee and Counselor Kim have taken up initiatives to contribute to the OECD's profile and relationship with regard to the upcoming G20 summits in Turkey (2015) and China (2016). These two summits provide a potential nexus for South Korean high-level policy interests in both the G20 and the United Nations, especially in its work under UN Secretary-General Ban Ki-moon's post-2015 sustainable development agenda.[8]

OECD Secretary-General Angel Gurria has made clear two priorities during his leadership. The first is partners—specifically, China,

India, Brazil, Indonesia, and South Africa—which are crucial to global outcomes and member country interests; and the second is the G20, which is important to OECD member countries' interests in the global economy, and therefore so is the OECD's role in relation to the G20 summit process, including meetings of G20 sherpas and finance deputies. As a result of the commitments outlined by Gurria, the OECD is widely respected for its substantive contributions to G20 summits, especially on structural reform but also on tax base erosion, finance, development, and the environment. Gurria is one of several leaders of international organizations who is seated at the G20 summit table; he is backed up by his longtime G20 sherpa, Gabriela Ramos, and recent G20 finance deputy and current OECD chief economist Catherine Mann, who replaced Pier Carlo Padoan when he became finance minister of Italy.

Ambassador Sihyung Lee initiated what may be a series of meetings on the subject of the OECD and global economic governance, including the orientation of the OECD over the next two years, during which time the Turkey and China G20 summits will be crucial to the effectiveness of such governance. By undertaking this initiative as representatives of an OECD member country, they are independently contributing to the understanding and involvement of all OECD delegations on G20 issues, processes, and deliberations, which increases the support within the membership for the OECD's G20 work.

This is a small but interesting case of a middle-power initiative within the context of the OECD membership of advanced industrial countries; South Korea's initiative adds value and generates respect and further influence for a country that is trying to advance its own interests by promoting institutional strengthening within the organizations of which it is a member. Again, the ROK's middle-power roles in the OECD and G20 illustrate how leadership and the initiative of individuals can make a difference in middle-power diplomacy effectiveness and outcomes.

INSTITUTIONS

Focusing on three South Korean leaders and their entrepreneurial efforts to deal with global challenges naturally highlights the degree to which the ROK's commitment to cultivating leaders and leadership is not only intentional but institutional. South Korea invested in education during its development drive, and this investment in human capital has contributed more to that development than was recognized by economists for many years. (Economists instead have tended to focus on investment-driven growth, capital output ratios, and neoclassical growth models that were based on the amount of labor and capital and in which technological change was exogenous.) Hence, skills and quality of labor were largely overlooked or embedded in the focus on productivity change induced by technology. Further, the ROK has a diverse set of high-quality universities that offer educations in science, technology, finance, business, and government.

But beyond the educational system, there are many institutions within South Korea that support leadership development, two of which, the Korea Foundation (KF) and the Korea Development Institute, stand out as significant contributors to the capacity of South Korea to serve successfully as a middle power.

Founded in 1991, KF is a publicly funded institution with an independent board of advisors. Its mission is "to promote better understanding of Korea within the international community and to increase friendship and good will between Korea and the rest of the world through various exchange programs."[9] This boilerplate does not adequately describe what is a highly intentional program—one that is meant to not only train South Koreans for international leadership, but also to include young professional South Koreans in relationships with their peers in other countries, which is carried out through individual exchanges and by bringing groups of emerging leaders from abroad to KF's seminars, conferences, and educational programs alongside young South Koreans.

KF represents a deliberate, intentional effort by South Korea to build the human capital and capacity needed to buttress and support the ROK's global reach and international leadership. One of the crucial components of being a successful middle power is to have a deep bench of human talent across an array of professions and sectors to undertake international leadership and global responsibility. KF is not the only contributor to creating the deep bench, but it plays a major role. An equivalent institution to KF is not found in many countries, and its presence may be one reason why there are not many other middle powers who can punch above their weight the way South Korea is able to do.

KDI was one of the first think tanks in a developing country to gain international recognition. It remains today a standard setter among global think tanks, making significant contributions not only within South Korea but also to global debates. It is large, well funded, and well managed. South Korea's best economic and financial researchers make up KDI's core staff, and the country's ability to play a leadership role in a knowledge-based global economy depends on think tanks like it.

CONCLUSIONS

Perhaps the most important issue for South Korea to figure out in its current pursuit of middle-power diplomacy is whether there are ways to ensure continuity across administrations of successive elected governments. Australia under Tony Abbott backed away from and reversed the climate change measures and leadership nurtured by Abbot's predecessor, Kevin Rudd. Canada under Stephen Harper did not own the G20 as a Canadian idea, instead downgrading it to a "Paul Martin idea," which weakened Canada's multilateral diplomacy, long a tradition for the North American middle power. South Korea's middle-power prominence has been accorded less foreign policy priority under President Park than it was under her predecessor, Lee. In particular, South Korean leadership on green growth and the G20 has noticeably waned—along with the ROK's standing as a middle power.

Tearing down the house that the previous administration built is not always necessary or desirable, despite best intentions by the government-elect to introduce new initiatives. Continuity of proactive middle-power diplomatic strategies and policies is important for maintaining middle-power status; influence derives in part from the coalitions, which should be formed through mutual trust of other middle powers' commitment to multilateralism and diplomacy. If countries run alternately hot and cold on middle-power assertiveness, the collective consensus among a faction of middle powers dwindles, which makes any sustainable coordinated action difficult, if not impossible.

From 2008 to mid-2012—the beginning of the global financial crisis through the Los Cabos G20 summit in Mexico—South Korea was able to establish collaborative relationships with other middle powers, including Australia, Canada, Mexico, the United Kingdom, and perhaps Vietnam and Indonesia. But for a variety of reasons, it is not so obvious now whether there is a cohort of collaborative middle powers that might enable South Korea to exercise leadership as a middle power or to exercise leadership collectively with a cluster of middle powers.

South Korea has a deep bench in terms of international talent and globally prepared private- and public-sector leaders. Drawing on this pool, South Korea can use its embassies and ambassadors and its positions on the boards of directors of other international institutions as instruments for exerting global leadership as a middle power. There is already established in the Ministry of Foreign Affairs a multilateral diplomacy coordinator and a directorate for multilateral economic diplomacy that contains the ministry's officials for the G20 and for international economic institutions. There would seem to be some high-yield gains for South Korea in coordinating its mission at the UN in New York with those in Washingon, Paris, and Geneva for issues related to international institutions and with those in the capitals of Mexico, Indonesia, Turkey, and Australia, which would provide opportunities for concerted leverage in the international institutions and in the G20. Linking these coordination efforts to working with and influencing the current G20 troika countries in 2015 and beyond of Australia, Turkey, and China—two MIKTA countries and a major trading partner next door—could be an experiment in multilateral middle-power diplomacy for South Korea. A MIKTA G20 sherpas' meeting was held in Seoul in February 2015—South Korea holds the chair for this year—which could also prove a promising effort, but it is too soon to evaluate its impact.

South Korea has a strong legacy interest in the UN's post-2015 development agenda because of its own exemplary performance as a dynamic economy, its national commitment to green growth, and its leadership of the UN by Ban Ki-moon during the development of the Sustainable Development Goals. Given its diplomatic strength at the UN and the OECD and its success as the G20 host in 2010, the ROK could now play a critical role in bridging the SDG goal-setting year, 2015, to the implementation phase that begins in 2016 under the G20 presidencies of Turkey and China.

South Korea could set an example for other countries by creating a Presidential Committee for Sustainable Development (PCSD), which would use the multisectoral and multiministerial experiences it has had with presidential committees as internal coordinating mechanisms. These "whole-of-government" efforts also involve important participants from the private sector, business, and finance. The PCSD could not only drive the integrated efforts required to achieve sustainability in South Korea's national trajectory, but also contribute to the post-2015 agenda follow-up process through data collection, monitoring, and evaluation; reporting; and providing feedback to South Korean policy-makers and the international institutions on the ROK's progress.

South Korea has been able to punch above its weight in the world due to its dynamic trajectory, strategic vision, historical narrative, leadership of individuals, and important supportive institutions. These national assets do not disappear or dissipate in a few years. They represent a foundation that can be drawn upon to assert global leadership when opportunities present themselves. South Korea's recent history of exemplary leadership in global governance and international institutions is surely not something this successful middle power would want to turn its back on in the future. Other middle powers and potential middle powers have much to learn from the Korean example. And the world as a whole has a stake in Korea's continuing to use its assets to assert global leadership in the years ahead, when stronger international leadership, global governance, and international institutions will be vital in addressing intensifying global challenges.

Development Effectiveness: Charting South Korea's Role and Contributions

*Brendan Howe**

Middle powers such as South Korea lack the capacity to influence global discourse across every dimension of international governance. As such, to maximize their relevance and impact, a degree of selectivity on the part of these middle powers is required, in terms of policy prioritization and/or geographical region. South Korea has grown from being one of the poorest countries in the world—it heavily depended on ODA for fifty years (1945–95)—to being in 2010 the newest member of the OECD DAC. The past two decades have also seen dramatic progress in political governance in the ROK. Enabled by a successful transition to democracy and democratic consolidation, South Korea now hosts many governance and development fact-finding missions. It also sponsors, through the Korean Overseas International Cooperation Agency (KOICA), the studies of large numbers of graduate students from small- and medium-size regional economies, who perhaps see in the ROK a role model closely analogous to their own conditions and experiences. Indeed, South Korea represents a postcolonial, conflict-affected, economic and political development success story, and thus serves as a remarkable source of inspiration to societies facing similar challenges.

Ranging from emergency relief to structural adjustment programs, ODA significantly contributed to South Korea's own economic and social development (in combination with South Korea's internal prioritization of human development in the realms of education and capacity building). In particular, ODA was the only available source of capital following the devastation of the ROK's economy by the Korean War. From 1945 to the early 1990s, South Korea received ODA from other

*The author would like to acknowledge research assistance from Seo Hyun Rachelle Park and thank the BK21 Plus Program for Global Networking Leadership Development and Education, Ewha Womans University GSIS, and the Freie Universität Berlin.

countries that amounted to $12 billion.[1] During the period of rapid economic growth from 1961 to 1975, more concessional loans and other forms of financial investment came to South Korea, allowing it to build social and economic infrastructure and promote industrial development. The "Miracle on the Han River" saw South Korea grow from one of the world's poorest countries—with a GDP per capita of $67 in 1953—to the world's fifteenth-largest economy. South Korea's economic growth can be seen, therefore, as having been fueled by foreign aid; in particular, beginning in the 1960s, ODA provided to South Korea acted like domestic capital, allowing the South Korean government to utilize the funds to support its industrial policies.[2]

A SHINING DEVELOPMENTAL CITY ON A HILL AND SHARING SUCCESS

In 1995, South Korea graduated from being an aid recipient when it paid off its final structural adjustment loan to the World Bank. It was removed from the OECD's list of recipient nations in 2000. South Korea represents a rare case of an ODA recipient success story: a country that has overcome the dual challenges of postconflict underdevelopment and insecurity, a "miracle" of economic and political governance development, and a country that embraces both macro and human-centered development in its policy prioritization. South Korea sees its own experience as an asset it can provide to other recipients of aid. Thus South Korea has become increasingly involved in the international development world and has also sought to export its lessons learned rather than be content to serve merely as a developmental shining city on the hill. South Koreans are justly proud of their success story and are keen to enhance their country's visibility by applying their own development experiences to the ROK's current aid programs to developing countries and thereby making a unique contribution.[3] Hence, "in search of a new, responsible global role in the twenty-first century, the South Korean government has announced that it will provide foreign aid with a 'South Korean Model of Development Cooperation' based upon its 'development experience' in the latter half of the twentieth century."[4] As early as 1977, the Ministry of Foreign Affairs and Trade of Korea (MOFAT) started providing technical cooperation to a number of developing countries.[5] Seoul has launched three major policy platforms—the

Knowledge Sharing Program, the Development Experience Exchange Program (DEEP), and the World Friends Korea volunteer organization—through which it hopes to influence the development experience of partner countries. It has also been involved in a number of collaborative efforts with international and domestic civil society organizations and groups.

From its inception, the KSP has been the flagship program through which Seoul has endeavored to share South Korean experience and expertise and to export the South Korean development model. The ROK's Ministry of Strategy and Finance (MOSF) launched the KSP as a "new paradigm of development cooperation" in 2004. It is advertised as a "knowledge-intensive development and economic cooperation program designed to share Korea's development experience with partner countries" that offers "comprehensive policy consultations tailored to the needs of partner countries encompassing in-depth analysis, policy consultation, and training opportunities."[6] Its three pillars are the Korea Development Institute (KDI), which leads policy consultation and system consulting (Bilateral KSP); the Export-Import Bank of Korea (Korea Eximbank), which leads joint consulting with international organizations (Multilateral KSP); and System Consulting and the KDI School, which leads modularization of Korea's development experience.[7] In 2011, the program partnered with twenty-five countries on KSP initiatives.[8] According to the KSP website, the number of country partners has since doubled. Policy areas include economic development strategy, industrialization and export promotion, economic crisis management, knowledge-based economy, and human-resource development.[9] By 2012, South Korea had successfully completed policy consultation for 107 countries on more than 440 topics. The KSP budget increased seventeenfold between 2004 and 2012,[10] and from 2012 to 2013, the KSP budget increased from 3.7 billion South Korean won to 5.7 billion won.[11] In 2012, the South Korean government launched the Multilateral KSP initiative, which is managed by the Korea Eximbank and primarily focuses on partnerships with regional and multilateral development banks such as the World Bank and the Asian Development Bank.[12]

In contrast to the KDI-administered Bilateral KSP, the Korean Overseas International Cooperation Agency (KOICA) runs DEEP. Although DEEP is based on knowledge transfer of South Korean expertise and experience (including two decades of KOICA ODA activities), it also looks to provide a dynamic transition model tailored to the specific needs of individual development partners and their operating environments.[13] KOICA invites government officials and policymakers from developing countries to participate in training courses and field trips; hence DEEP is implemented through three different pillars: participatory consulting, result-oriented consulting, and comprehensive consulting.[14] The KOICA training program aims to share important technical skills and knowledge as well as build capacities for sustainable development.[15] Every year, about four thousand people from developing countries are trained in South Korea, while South Korean experts and volunteers are sent into the field to transfer the development experience. In 2009, the South Korean government and the United Nations Development Program (UNDP) signed an agreement to establish a Policy Center on Global Development Partnerships in Seoul.[16] Since 1991, KOICA has offered more than two thousand courses on sectors such as education, governance, rural development, and information and communications technology and has trained 44,321 people from 173 developing countries. KOICA supports fully funded master's degree programs at Korean universities in order to provide long-term, continuous, and sustainable training environments. Every year, approximately 290 participants from developing countries (usually junior government officials) at fifteen universities in South Korea are funded to participate in long-term research programs leading to professional master's degrees.

In 1989, the South Korean government announced the inauguration of its overseas volunteer program, and the following year the UNESCO Korean National Committee dispatched the first batch of volunteers to four Asian countries. In 1991, the program came under the auspices of KOICA and was expanded to seven countries.[17] Other volunteer programs followed, including the Korea Internet Volunteers (in which volunteers taught about technology) under the Ministry of Public Administration and Security; the Korea University Volunteers (a short-term program for university students to offer service opportunities of a few weeks to five months); and the Korea Techno Peace Corps (which had one-year assignments), the latter two run by the Ministry of Science, Education, and Technology.[18] In 2009, the Lee Myung-bak administration brought these programs and a number of others together to form World Friends Korea. Each year, an additional one thousand volunteers join the sixteen hundred already in the field in the regular program, and an additional several hundred serve in more ad hoc programs for a total of more than three thousand people deployed annually.[19] World Friends Korea's objectives are "to improve the quality of life of residents in developing countries; to increase cooperation and mutual understanding between developing countries and Korea; [and] to achieve self-realization and growth through service activities."[20] The ROK is one of only six countries that has such an overseas volunteer program (the others are Belgium, Germany, Japan, Luxembourg, and the United States), and South Korea's program is second only to the United States' in terms of size.[21]

In addition to setting an example to be followed and disseminating expertise and experience, South Korea has also, in recent years, become a major donor of ODA and contributor to the international discourse on and management of ODA.

AN INCREASINGLY IMPORTANT CONTRIBUTOR

South Korea became a donor of ODA in 1963, when it was asked by the U.S. Agency for International Development (USAID) to participate in a joint training project. It was not, however, until the late 1980s and early 1990s that South Korea became an independent donor of ODA. In 1987, after South Korea had enjoyed nearly three decades of rapid industrialization, it established the Economic Development Cooperation Fund (EDCF) under the Korea Eximbank to handle concessional loans. KOICA was established in 1991 to deal with grant aid. Since joining the OECD in 1996 and the DAC in 2010, South Korea has worked hard to boost its aid and to contribute to global development efforts.

Even before joining the OECD DAC, however, "Korea had emerged as the unrivalled leading donor, in absolute amounts, among non-DAC OECD countries."[22] What makes South Korea stand out is its ODA activism, which should be seen in the context of South Korea's experience of initially being an aid recipient nation, allowing it to provide aid from the recipient's perspective.[23] This ODA activism initially emerged under the Lee administration in the guise of "contribution diplomacy," which imagined ODA as a means to "contribute to global peace and development under a broader vision and a more proactive approach to interacting with the international community" and was considered a rare attempt by the South Korean government to take up global issues

in its diplomatic agenda. The Park Geun-hye administration later combined development cooperation with middle-power diplomacy.[24] The
president's office delegated the planning of this development cooperation strategy to MOFAT, which quickly identified four main diplomatic
tasks for development cooperation: "(1) Security diplomacy, particularly on the Korean peninsula; (2) Diplomacy that contributes to global
co-prosperity; (3) Diplomacy that secures engines for future growth,
particularly through trade and co-operation in the fields of energy and
resources; (4) Diplomacy that serves the public, particularly the needs
of Koreans abroad."[25]

By the time of the first DAC peer review of Korea in 2012, the country had trebled its ODA over the preceding five years to $1,325 mil-
lion per year, or 0.12 percent of its gross national income (GNI), and it
had committed to a further doubling by 2015.[26] In 2012, Korea's ODA
amounted to $1,597.5 million (net disbursement), of which $1,183.2
million was bilateral aid and $414.3 million was multilateral aid.
Grants amounted to $714.9 million (60.4 percent) and loans to $468.3
million (39.6 percent) of the total; KOICA provided $444.5 million
the same year.[27] In fact, in 2012, under conditions of financial crisis,
South Korea had the largest increase in ODA among the DAC at 17
percent, far ahead of Australia's 9.2 percent, the next largest increase;
most DAC members decreased their ODA that year.[28] From 2006 to
2013, Korea's ODA budget more than tripled, from $440 million to
$1.67 billion in 2013.[29] Prime Minister Jung Hong-won committed in
January 2014 to spending more than $2 billion on ODA over the fol-
lowing twelve months, an 11 percent increase from the previous year
and a step closer to keeping the promise of making foreign aid 0.25
percent of the country's GNI by 2015. According to Minho Cho, the
country's ODA bureau deputy director, "We are taking efforts to
increase steadily the size of our ODA for several years and we are planning to increase [it more] going forward, we are committed to making
our 0.25 percent [of GNI] commitment by 2015."[30] It seems South
Korea fell just short of these targets—its total annual ODA, including
grants, credit assistance through the Eximbank, and economic development cooperation funds reached 2 trillion won (about $1.92 billion)
in 2014, of which 622.6 billion won (about $598.3 million) was ODA.
A 9 percent jump was earmarked for 2015,[31] but this was subsequently
reduced to 5 percent.[32] The DAC peer review had many positive things
to say about Korean ODA performance:

Since joining the Development Assistance Committee (DAC) in January 2010, Korea has worked hard to strengthen its aid and to contribute to global development efforts. Korea's DAC membership followed an extensive accession process and a special session of the DAC on 25 November 2009. At this meeting, members expressed genuine admiration for Korea's success in transforming itself from an aid recipient (as recently as 1995) to an important aid donor in such a short space of time. Korea is now seen by developing countries, particularly those in East Asia, as a source of knowledge and ideas on development drawn from actual experience. This is an area of particular comparative advantage relative to other DAC members.[33]

In 2010, South Korea strengthened its legal framework for a more effective ODA system by enacting the Framework Act on International Development Cooperation, which lays out the principles, objectives, and coordination mechanism of Korea's ODA. In October of that year, the Committee for International Development Cooperation (CIDC) chaired by the prime minister, adopted the Strategic Plan for International Development Cooperation, which outlined major strategies and plans to strengthen South Korea's capacity as a development partner, including "systematically documenting the development contents of successes and failures derived from Korea's development experience, strengthening ODA implementing capacities, and taking a proactive role in addressing global issues."[34] In addition to strengthening the framework for its own development assistance, South Korea participated in international debates and global process.[35] The country hosted the G20 summit in 2010 and played a leading role in expanding the G20 agenda to include development issues, while during the Fourth High Level Forum on Aid Effectiveness (HLF-4) at Busan in 2011, the ROK paved the way to enhancing global partnership between DAC members and recipients.[36]

South Korea's 2010 hosting of the G20 summit, the premier forum for international economic cooperation, represented the first opportunity for Seoul to set a global agenda. From the outset, South Korea made clear its intent to prominently feature development issues in the global economic policy discussions. Much was made of the concept of South Korea serving as a bridge between the developing and developed worlds as a result of its own experience and expertise, and the forum also offered Seoul the opportunity to stimulate a recommitment to the Millennium Development Goals (MDGs) as the global agreed-upon framework for development leading up to 2015.[37] Korea promoted the Seoul Development Consensus for Shared Growth and its Multi-Year Action Plan on Development during the Seoul summit, ensuring that the G20 development agenda would be tailored to help developing countries build capacity in important areas toward sustainable and inclusive economic growth.[38] The following year, South Korea served as co-chair of the G20 development working group and therefore played a major role in implementing the G20 development agenda. Then, at the 2011 Cannes summit, "the G20 identified major bottlenecks to development in developing countries and provided solutions in crucial pillars including 'infrastructure' and 'food security.'"[39]

It was, however, at the HLF-4, which took place in the South Korean port city of Busan from November 29 through December 1, 2011, that the ROK made a serious impression as a middle power in the niche area of development assistance. More than two thousand representatives from government, civil society, and business came from both developed and developing countries to discuss the current global development assistance situation, giving the ROK government the opportunity to comprehensively reframe the international development debate.[40] Although it is premature to argue that a new paradigm was established at Busan, there was clear political momentum for a shift from aid effectiveness to development effectiveness, advocated and promoted in particular by new actors such as South Korea, and South Korea has "attempted to play an important middle power role in global development cooperation through the HLF and post-HLF processes."[41] The goals pursued at Busan included assessing the aid effectiveness paradigm in development cooperation; moving toward the new paradigm of development effectiveness; and transforming the HLF to become a more inclusive process in order to retain its legitimacy as a global forum for development cooperation.[42] The achievements of the South Korean government's chairing of the Busan HLF in pursuit of these goals were numerous.

South Korea both hosted the discussions and led the direction of the negotiations. The ROK successfully integrated the BRIC countries (Brazil, Russia, India, and China), to an unprecedented extent, into a new global platform for aid discussions, and also served as arbitrator between the developed and developing countries.[43] "Fully utilizing its diplomatic resources such as G20 and UN Secretary-General Ban

Ki-Moon, Korea endeavored to prevent polarization during discussions between the developed and developing countries."[44] Indeed, South Korea was able to secure agreement among traditional donors and emerging economies on the language of "common goals" but "differential commitments" while also promoting the inclusion of gender empowerment in the Busan outcome document.[45] Busan was by far the most inclusive HLF on aid effectiveness. Not only did the official senior representatives of high-, middle-, and low-income countries, new and old donors and recipients, and international organizations attend in unprecedented numbers, but nongovernmental organizations (NGOs) and private corporations were also present. Therefore, although the earlier HLFs had been criticized for being dominated by donors and their agendas, the Busan HLF-4 was complimented for the much broader partnership and its "New Deal" for fragile states.[46] Thus a truly global partnership for the effective implementation of development assistance was initiated with the aim of extending transparency, accountability, and verifiability.[47] The final outcome document, the Busan Partnership Document, called, therefore, for a "new, inclusive, and representative Global Partnership for Effective Development Cooperation to support and ensure accountability for the implementation of commitments."[48]

The shift in development cooperation from financial aid and aid effectiveness to the promotion of economic growth, development effectiveness, and knowledge sharing was the most significant element of the ROK's issue leadership—and this also reflected South Korea's own interests.[49] In the context of this paradigmatic shift, "comprehensive issues of development cooperation such as South-South and triangular cooperation, effective institutions and capacity development, gender equality and women's empowerment, climate finance, and the public-private partnership were re-examined."[50] Busan represented a shift from questions of how to give and use aid more effectively toward those of "'How will aid deliver development?' and 'What other factors besides aid contribute to development?'"[51] Again, this shift would appear to be reflective of the South Korean model and South Korean interests. As in common with other Asian donors, South Korea tends to view development cooperation as part of a more comprehensive development partnership package that includes aid, loans, trade, and foreign direct investment (FDI).[52]

Along with building cooperative links with Asian, BRIC, and developing countries, South Korea has worked to bring its ODA practices more in line with DAC guidelines and to build partnerships with European donors. In early March 2009, President Lee announced the New Asia Initiative, intended to enhance Korea's cooperation with neighboring Asian countries, including a plan for increasing ODA contributions to developing countries in Asia.[53] The South Korean government has been described as playing a pivotal role in sub-Saharan Africa, in close collaboration with the private sector: "The Korea-Africa Forum, the Korea-Africa Economic Cooperation, and the Korea-Africa Industry Cooperation Forum underpin this strategy."[54] In contrast to Japan, which prioritizes upper-middle-income countries including China and Indonesia, and in line with DAC recommendations to prioritize aid to the least developed countries and low-income countries, all of Korea's five largest ODA recipients are classified as low-income or lower-middle-income countries by the World Bank. Indeed, in 2010, Korea allocated 61 percent of its gross bilateral ODA to these two groups of countries, which is above the DAC average of 53 percent and Japan's 23 percent.[55]

In addition to bilateral-cooperation initiatives with various European countries, in 2010 the EU–South Korea Framework Agreement committed the two parties to strengthening cooperation in the area of development assistance. Thus cooperation on international development has been identified as a promising issue for the future agenda of the Korea-EU partnership.[56] South Korea's rise was also underlined by the World Bank's decision to establish a new office in Incheon. According to the bank's regional director, Klaus Rohland, the Korean office will extend the Washington, DC–based institution's mission to assist developing nations in the region by sharing South Korea's success story as the country "plays an increasingly active role in global development issues."[57]

CAVEATS, CRITICISMS, AND CHALLENGES GOING FORWARD

The first caveat is that Korea's own development experience has its limitations, which, therefore, constrains the extent to which it can suitably be transferred to others. Much of the literature on the South Korean "miracle," in some instances seemingly little more than government propaganda, relates a sanitized version of South Korea's modern history. Outside the issue of shortchanging factual and

multifaceted accounts of Korean history, there are three policy problems related to these versions of Korean history. Incomplete represen-
tation of the South Korean model raises questions of its desirability
and the actual efficacy of some of the Korean development policies.
Second, a singular South Korean case casts doubt on the degree to
which any success stories actually reflected the impact and successful
utilization of ODA, which may instead have been primarily a response
to environmental considerations. Third, such propaganda itself plays
a complex role in enabling or undermining middle-power activism
and warrants further consideration.

There is no doubt that to achieve its development objectives, the
South Korean dictatorship sacrificed the human rights of its people.
There remains, however, a disturbing trend of authoritarianism in
some political circles and an ongoing tendency to sacrifice individuals
for the collective good. At a minimum, Korean policymakers continue
to promote technocratic approaches rather than human-centered
ones. This is in direct contradiction to the evolving international
consensus on human rights and goes against the modern development agenda outlined in the Paris Declaration and the Accra Agenda
for Action. Authoritarian leaders and governments may take heart
from the South Korean experience and approach, but it is certainly
not likely to set the global agenda alight. Among the development programs pursued under the Park Chung-hee regime, the New Village
Movement (*Saemaul Undong*) is one that is now being championed by
his daughter's administration for export to other countries. In October 2014, about 450 people from forty countries took part in the first
Global Saemaul Leadership Forum 2014 in Seongnam, Gyeonggi-do,
one of the four provinces that also hosts Saemaul Undong Central
Training Institutes.[58] This program has been lauded for improvements
in basic infrastructure but criticized for a relatively limited influence on
poverty reduction and socioeconomic development.[59] These concrete
construction projects in rural communities also had significant detri-
mental effects on the human and natural environment. Similar concerns can be raised with regard to South Korean attempts to export its
development model, as explored further in the following pages.

As noted earlier, during each of its periods of economic growth,
South Korea received significant ODA impetus from other countries in the form of both grants and concessional loans, allowing it
to build social and economic infrastructure and promote industrial

development. South Korea's aid experience can be categorized into five distinct stages: the 1945–48 period of early, post–World War II foreign assistance, primarily from the United States; the 1949–60 period of foreign assistance aimed at state-building and reconstruction; the 1961–75 period, representing the middle stage of foreign assistance that was focused on boosting economic and social development (and was also supported by Japanese reparations following the normalization of relations in 1965); the 1976–90 period, characterized as a late stage of foreign assistance designed for a modern industrialized economy; and the 1991–99 period of transformation from a recipient to a donor.[60] In each stage, South Korea has pursued different economic development strategies, and the roles and types of ODA have varied. It is not certain, however, that such an ODA recipient experience can or should be replicated. The first period of development assistance to South Korea was boosted by the presence of an occupying power that provided most of the grants. The second was characterized primarily by grants and unconditional ODA, the relative absence of which in South Korea's own assistance programs has led to international criticism. It also included emergency assistance as the country was wracked by civil war. The third depended not only on reparations from the former colonial power, but also from the tremendous boost the South Korean economy received from U.S. involvement in wars in Southeast Asia. Although South Korea has been praised for its ability to retain ownership of the development process, on the expenditure of funds received, and on capacity development, these are also prerogatives Seoul is accused of denying to recipients of its own largesse.[61]

By emphasizing its own development achievements in its dealings with other states, South Korea has been participating in an activity that under the current administration would probably be considered the promotion of public diplomacy. At its most strategic, and basic, formulation—linked to the concepts of soft power, propaganda, and national branding—public diplomacy is essentially about the pursuit of national interest through alternative diplomatic means, or in combination with traditional diplomacy. By combining public diplomacy based on soft-power assets and traditional diplomacy, it is hoped that a nation can achieve its goal of enhancing its national image and increase its influence in a manner favorable on the global stage.[62] Clearly this has much in common with the related concepts of middle power and niche diplomacy. Yet the propagandistic nature of such policy formulation and the terminology of soft power can backfire. Indeed, "one irony of soft power is that the theory emphasizes the importance of attraction in world affairs but presents that attraction as a mechanism for getting one's way, which is potentially an unattractive objective."[63] Even the overt use of the term "Korean Model of Development" is problematic because it implies "'one size fits all'—a singular mode of development—which does not fit with the global norms on foreign aid and development cooperation that recognize diverse developmental contexts of recipient nations."[64] By placing an emphasis on the South Korean model, there is a risk that Seoul's policies will be viewed as self-centeredness deriving from overconfidence in the country's own development success, and it might be "received as arrogance unless carefully executed."[65] Partly this is a problem of communication, and partly it is a result of fragmented "voice."

The second set of caveats concerns the fact that despite recent efforts and a willingness to take a leading role in the international development world, South Korea faces serious challenges and criticisms in terms of its ODA volume. South Korean aid topped only $500 million in the mid-2000s, and although it reached $1.325 billion in 2011, this was only equivalent to 0.12 percent of its GNI.[66] South Korea's ODA volume in 2011 was 6 percent greater than in 2010, but when its aid surpassed $1 billion for the first time, its ODA/GNI ratio was unchanged from 2010 and below DAC members' average of 0.32 percent as well as its target of 0.13 percent for the year. South Korea committed to increase the total volume of ODA to about $3 billion and ODA/GNI to 0.25 percent by 2015, but this has not been achieved. South Korea's total volume of ODA and its ODA/GNI ratio remain relatively small when compared with other traditional donor countries in North America, western Europe, and, in particular, the Nordic countries. Indeed, South Korea has been ranked at or near the bottom of many quantitative measurements of the ODA of DAC member countries. These include total ODA, ODA-GNI ratio, bilateral aid–ODA ratio, grants-ODA ratio, humanitarian grants–ODA ratio, multilateral aid–ODA ratio, and the Commitment to Development Index, comprising the seven areas of aid, trade, investment, technology, environment, migration, and security.[67]

These figures need not necessarily be viewed as purely negative. South Korea has, at least, been improving its performance across all of these measurements, while traditional donors are backing off from previous commitments and exhibiting signs of "donor fatigue." In fact, the

2008 financial crisis "precipitated a gradual retreat of 'traditional' Western donors from the center-stage of development aid, and has begun to place new actors closer to the spotlight."[68] Furthermore, considering ODA from the perspective of a middle power's interests, and given the amount of coverage and international prestige South Korea has generated through its aid activities (in particular the hosting of prestigious international conferences), relatively small financial contributions translate into much greater return.

A third caveat with regard to South Korea's middle-power role in the field of ODA governance, agenda setting, and policymaking is related to the disconnected commitment across South Korean administrations. There appears to have been little effort made to maintain the ODA agenda-setting momentum, which perhaps reached a climax with the Busan HLF. The transitional shift from aid effectiveness to development effectiveness has never been sufficiently explained, developed, or consistently pursued. Indeed, there is little material to be found reporting—let alone supporting—the concept of South Korean commitment to ODA after the 2012 OECD DAC peer review. Even the wider vision of Global Korea has fallen by the wayside under the current Park administration. The KSP, formerly the flagship program for sharing South Korea's development experience and expertise with the world (and therefore a central plank of South Korean attempts as a middle power to pursue an alternative niche strategic policy for the promotion of interests) is likewise out of favor. The current administration favors the term "public diplomacy," and when this author talked to senior government officials within the relevant government branches, the role of the former public-relations jewel, the KSP, was downplayed, or even discredited simply because it was administered by a competing agency and previous administration. Instead of development cooperation being mainstreamed throughout the government, including as a potential major contributor to South Korean public diplomacy, there is a danger it will become sidelined due to political infighting or short attention spans in the ROK government. South Korean ODA policymaking is subject to the vagaries of faddism and fractured governance.

The fourth caveat involves the geopolitical distribution of South Korean aid. The ROK has been criticized for narrowly focusing on Asia in its ODA distributions[69] as well as for bilateral rather than multilateral aid.[70] Certainly it is true that a large share of South Korea's aid has been and continues to be directed to Asia to strengthen development cooperation with regional partners. According to the Strategic Plan and the Mid-term ODA Policy for 2011–2015, which describe strategic orientations and allocation principles for each region, strategic priority is given to the Asian region.[71] Although South Korea recognizes the importance of Africa in its commitment to join the global efforts to fight poverty through the UN MDGs, the ROK has closer ties with Asian countries due to geographical proximity and cultural familiarity. Of twenty-six priority partner countries, eleven are located in Asia, and South Korea pledges to increase its aid to these Asian partner countries to 55 percent of all ROK bilateral aid by 2015.[72] Since the start of South Korea's official aid program in 1987, the largest amount of aid has been given to Vietnam, followed by Indonesia, Sri Lanka, Bangladesh, and Cambodia.[73] The ROK's top fifteen recipients include all of the poorest East Asian countries, and only one, Angola, is from a continent other than Asia.

Asia reportedly has been earmarked to receive 47 percent, Africa 17 percent, South America 6 percent, and the Middle East and the Commonwealth of Independent States about 5.5 percent of South Korean ODA funds, which are to be distributed through various channels (KOICA as well as multilateral partners), but the bulk of new funds will be distributed bilaterally.[74] As a result, therefore, critics have often identified South Korean aid as "flag aid," aimed more at advancing the visibility or image of the donor country than at achieving development in the recipient country.[75] Again, from a strategic perspective, these statistics may not represent a negative for the ROK.

Given the strategic limitations of middle powers in influencing international debates, it may seem to make sense to have a regional rather than a global geographical focus. Thus "although aid to other regions is important, as Korea scales up its giving it should stay focused on East Asia, an area in which it has a comparative advantage."[76] Likewise, given that middle-power activism is all about visibility on the international stage, it is not surprising that South Korea clings to bilateralism rather than multilateralism: when ODA is distributed by one single international organization, the visibility of the individual provider nation is reduced, which contradicts the aims of the Global Korea strategy.[77] International guidelines for aid effectiveness, such as the Paris and Accra road maps, recommend multilateral approaches, but considering the more than thirty donors per recipient country and the strong competition for recognition this entails, South Korea is likely, from its strategic perspective, to predominantly continue to go it alone. Recipients may even benefit from this prioritization, because the ROK will want to retain its highly visible regional profile—especially in the face of competition from Japan and China—and will therefore show greater commitment. At the least, recipients may feel more comfortable working with a regional development partner that shares similar experiences and values than with a European or North American donor that brings potential imperial or neoimperial baggage. Ironically, the final area of criticism of the dispersal of South Korean aid revolves around too great a dilution of aid to too many partners, and too many (more than one thousand) small projects.[78] If the ROK were to follow guidelines to reduce its number of development partners and projects, it is possible that this would lead to even further regional concentration.

Yet such focus on bilateral strategic relationships over multilateral collective efforts related to the global commons contradicts common conceptions of successful middle powers, particularly in terms of agenda setting and reputation building. For instance, the perception of the factors behind recent ROK involvement with sub-Saharan Africa are the pursuit of South Korean food and energy security; the establishment of new markets for its manufactured goods; and strategic competition with other East Asian actors, particularly China, in a new "scramble for Africa."[79] Indeed, South Korean government and media outlets also tend to present developing nations as either charitable objects or new economic frontiers, which leads critics to argue that such behavior goes against "Seoul's much-heralded moral obligation to voluntarily fulfill universal norms and values of liberty, justice, and humanitarianism/benevolence."[80] Middle powers need to go beyond narrowly defined national interests to accommodate other actors' interests "to organize the global governance of development cooperation by linking multiple fora."[81] Thus there are also reputational costs despite potential traditional strategic gains in the unilateralism of South Korean ODA.

Other theorists have pointed out that "middle power states have most recently been defined by their internationalism. States that exhibit certain foreign policy behavior are considered middle powers. Qualifying behavior might include good 'global citizenship,' niche diplomacy, and accepting roles as mediators, followers, or staunch multilateralists."[82] From this perspective, status as a middle power is conferred in accordance with behavior rather than size. Middle-power activism is all about visibility on the international stage, but it is also about playing by the rules of the global normative consensus and demonstrating a willingness to be a good global citizen.

There is a further danger that South Korea's political capital in the field, built up through the conference diplomacy of hosting the G20 and the HLF-4, could be dissipated through lack of multilateral follow-up and commitment and a too-obvious pursuit of narrow bilateral national interest. This could jeopardize South Korea's ability and opportunity to play a major role in the post-2015 agenda concerning the UN discussions on Sustainable Development Goals. These arguments spill over into the fifth, and perhaps most controversial set of caveats concerning the ROK's role and contributions as a middle power in the field of development effectiveness: the nature of South Korean aid.

Historically, much of South Korea's aid has been tied, or given on condition that it be spent on goods or services provided by South Korean interests. In 2006, as much as 98 percent of the ROK's aid was estimated as being tied or partially tied.[83] In 2007, some progress appeared to have been made, with as much as 25 percent of South Korean aid being untied, but this was still well below the OECD DAC member average.[84] Consequently, as "part of its accession to the DAC and its commitment to the Paris Declaration principles and the Accra Agenda for Action, in 2009 Korea put a timetable in place to increase the untied portion of its bilateral ODA to 75 percent by 2015."[85] By the time of the OECD DAC peer review in 2012, however, it was noted that South Korea had in fact made no progress toward this aim, but rather, "the untied proportion of Korea's total aid was lower in 2010 (at 32 percent) than in 2009 (44 percent)."[86] South Korea has also been criticized for the high percentage of concessional loans rather than grants in its assistance.[87] This is because loans can increase the recipients' susceptibility to debt undermining growth.[88] Yet with the 2010 reform plan for the ROK's international development cooperation forecasting maintenance of the composition of loans and grants at 40 percent and 60 percent until 2015, South Korea could again be perceived as unresponsive to international criticism and resistant to international best practices.[89]

Finally, South Korea has been criticized for focusing unduly on infrastructure and macroeconomic growth at the expense of social welfare in a manner that not only reflects the country's own development experience but also its ongoing interests (such as access to resources and markets and outgoing FDI).[90] According to Minho Cho, the deputy government director for official development assistance, infrastructure prioritization is likely to continue.[91] There has been some progress toward social welfare development assistance. Although more than half of South Korea's assistance has been directed toward areas such as economic infrastructure and production sectors, in the past decade the economic infrastructure sector has accounted for 37 percent whereas the share of South Korea's ODA for the social infrastructure sector is 46 percent, which is 15 percentage points higher than the overall average of DAC members (Figure 1). During the five years after 2002, in particular, two-thirds of South Korean aid was targeted toward the social sector, the field most closely associated with the provision of human-centered security and development. This large increase in the proportion of aid allocated to social infrastructure since the early 2000s is mainly due to an increase in water supply, health, government, and civil-society initiatives in response to the global commitment to the MDGs.[92]

According to the EDCF's 2003 annual report, development goals included "economic development and industrialization of developing countries" by "sharing Korea's development experience and transferring technological expertise accumulated during its economic development."[93] By 2004, the emphasis had shifted to the sustainable development of partner countries and South Korea's participation in development efforts, such as the MDGs.[94] This emphasis on sustainable development led South Korea to place higher priority on improving people's quality of life by providing forms of social infrastructure in sectors such as the water supply, public health, and education.[95] Eventually, investments in social infrastructure topped those in economic

FIGURE 1. SOUTH KOREAN LOAN COMMITMENTS IN 2013

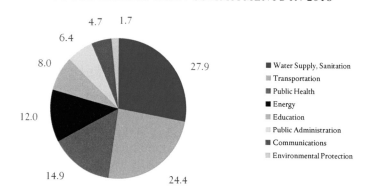

Source: EDCF 2013 annual report.

infrastructure—the three aforementioned sectors accounted for 50.8 percent of total loan commitments in 2013, whereas the total share of commitments in economic sectors such as transportation (24.4 percent), energy (12.1 percent), and communication (4.7 percent) totaled merely 41.2 percent of loan commitments.[96] Therefore, compared with countries such as Japan, whose aid overwhelmingly continues to support building economic infrastructure, South Korea could be seen as having development priorities much closer to DAC norms, which allows it to focus on social development.

Nonetheless, even as the ROK places social infrastructural development at the top of its agenda, it has placed an ongoing subsector emphasis on economic infrastructure development. Hence, a significant amount of its loans were also allocated to crucial economic infrastructure sectors such as transportation, energy, and telecommunication (Figure 2).

In 2013, South Korea's investment in transportation increased because the government was confident that improved transportation networks would contribute to growth and balanced economic development. Hence, that sector has been allocated the most aid: investments totaled 18.5 percent of bilateral aid in 2012 and 15.8 percent of total ODA in 2014.[97] In addition, South Korea has strongly preferred financing the building of basic hard infrastructure over that of social services, budget support, and humanitarian aid. For example, in 2002, when the social infrastructure sector accounted for 63 percent of bilateral ODA,

FIGURE 2. SOUTH KOREAN LOAN DISBURSEMENTS IN 2013

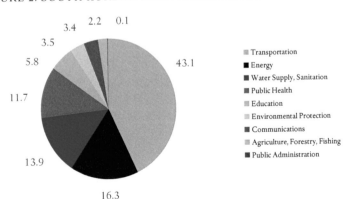

Source: EDCF 2013 annual report.

education assistance took up 43 percent of social sector allocation.[98] In 2013, however, when the social infrastructure sector accounted for 43.8 percent of bilateral ODA commitments, education assistance dropped to 7.3 percent.[99] This type of aid aimed at increasing physical capital is classified as project-type interventions by OECD, and South Korea has provided more than 60 percent of bilateral aid as project-type interventions since 1987.[100]

Thus the ROK has attempted to balance investments in both social and economic infrastructure by concentrating on the transportation, water and sanitation, and education sectors. South Korea also sought to expand ODA for emergency relief while primarily giving project-based aid (67.5 percent). From these two findings, it can be said that South Korea's ODA priorities have not undergone radical change. This is reflective of South Korea's own development experience whereby the foundations for growth were first laid by concentrating ODA to social and economic infrastructure projects.[101] For some, all this adds up to a tendency to favor the interests of the donor over the recipient.[102] Even South Korea's performance at the Busan HLF-4 did not meet with universal acclaim—criticism of economic-oriented terminology and the ROK's focus on economic development models, lack of emphasis on the potential detriment of private-sector participation, vagueness regarding crucial issues such as untied aid, and absence of human rights, including gender equality, was added to the Busan Outcome Document.[103] The new governance structure presented in Busan represented significant progress in inclusiveness, but also represented "a burden on the ability to promote tangible and meaningful collective action as the number and diversity of decision makers" grew.[104] As a result, for instance, on the important issue of tied aid, nothing proved possible beyond a general commitment to make progress, and no deadline was attached.

In fact, many of South Korea's current development projects suffer from a lack of accountability, oversight, and consultation with partners. In part this is due to the fragmentation of South Korean ODA, which constitutes a sixth serious set of caveats concerning the ROK's middle-power activism in the field of ODA. South Korean development assistance policymaking has long faced the challenges of intragovernmental coordination at home—there is much fragmentation between the prime minister's office, the two core ministries (MOFAT and MOSF), KOICA, the Eximbank, and indeed thirty to forty other relevant institutions.[105] In its 2008 special review of the ROK, the DAC recommended that the

South Korean government establish "a single entity with sole authority over development cooperation objectives, policy, and strategy," but by the 2012 peer review, despite the establishment of the CIDC, the DAC again advised South Korea to create a government-wide agenda to achieve coherent, sufficient, development-friendly policies.[106] The peer review further recommended the CIDC use its powers fully to become the ultimate decision-making body in planning and budgeting processes, and that the "Inter-Agency Committees, together with the ODA Councils at partner country level, have the necessary authority to ensure that all aid-funded activities are processed through them."[107]

Indeed, there remains something of an academic consensus on the lack of a coherent development philosophy or strategy behind South Korea's ODA.[108] Part of the reputational damage discussed above stems from poor communication and policy presentation by the ROK, such as overtly using the term "soft power" on official websites and in policy documents dedicated to the promotion of South Korean assistance. Throughout the peer review process carried out with regard to Korea by other members of the OECD DAC, concerns have been raised about reporting and transparency of South Korean development activities. Yet few government reports have come out since the publication of the OECD DAC peer review because the fragmentation of official reporting bodies makes locating a comprehensive set of extant reports difficult. Again, as pointed out by the OECD DAC peer review, there is no budget or supplementary documentation that clearly sets out South Korea's aid expenditure in each country and sector and that is easily accessible to everyone, thus the relevant bodies should increase transparency and accountability by providing comprehensive information on the ROK's development cooperation in a way that is "easy for key stakeholders—parliamentarians, civil society organizations (CSOs), non-government organizations (NGOs), private sector, research institutes, developing country partners, and the general public—to access and understand."[109] Voices in the South Korean aid community, notably in civil society, have also campaigned for more accountable and efficient South Korean aid, most recently advocating that the ROK join the International Aid Transparency Initiative.[110] Without such a degree of transparency and adequate reporting, not only will South Korea miss the opportunity to broadcast achievements and influence international discourse to the fullest of its ability, but there is also a chance that its government will lose domestic support for related policies.[111]

CONCLUSIONS

The rapidly shifting nature of development cooperation in the twenty-first century presents middle powers with a "noble opportunity" to do something that is both normatively right and beneficial to others while also in the national interest; these changes have coincided with "South Korea's ambitious launch of its middle power diplomacy strategy."[112] The ROK has a number of comparative advantages in fulfilling this role: it comes to the table without any imperial or neoimperial legacy, from a non-Western and nonhegemonic perspective; poses little threat to the sovereignty of developing partner countries; and is able to set a significant example to others in terms of both experience and expertise in transforming from a developing to a developed state, from an aid recipient to a donor, and from an authoritarian regime to a consolidated democracy—and all in the context of ongoing security challenges.

As a new donor, South Korea can be considered immune from the sins of the past (i.e., colonization and previously discredited aid policies) and is also potentially less susceptible to aid fatigue among its own population, due to enthusiasm for the ROK to play an enhanced role on the global stage and to "pay back" for previous assistance. The country is therefore uniquely positioned to punch above its weight in this strategic operating environment by providing a bridge between developing and developed nations, between donors and recipients, between North and South, and between East and West.

Care has to be taken, however, to not squander this opportunity and to maintain support for South Korea's enhanced role both within the country and in the wider international discourse and operating environment. To date, the ROK has missed opportunities to establish the ongoing bureaucratic mechanisms and human-resource contributions through which it could have a lasting influence on the issue areas concerned. It needs therefore to finally implement some of the recommendations of the OECD DAC peer review in terms of bureaucratic consolidation, but it also needs to normalize development cooperation throughout its policymaking, thereby insulating it against the vagaries of administrational change. In terms of policy content, again in accordance with peer review recommendations, the ROK needs to follow contemporary international norms more closely, in particular with regard to developing multilateral collaborative aid partnerships, untying aid and phasing out concessional loans altogether in favor of grants, focusing on human development rather than infrastructure, and owning the ODA process and agenda setting by recipient countries.

These policy changes and initiatives need to be communicated in a more effective manner than they have been, not only in the interests of transparency and accountability as demanded by both NGOs and the peer review, but also because in doing so, South Korea can further its own public diplomatic interests. Only by acting in accordance with international development assistance norms, playing the role of a good global citizen, cooperating with others, and allowing others to sing South Korea's praises rather than blowing its own horn can the ROK hope to achieve the agenda-setting role of a middle power in the global discourse.

Nuclear Governance: South Korea's Efforts to Strengthen Regimes and Frameworks for the Safe and Secure Use of Nuclear Energy

Toby Dalton

South Korea stands in a unique position among the global nuclear elite: it is the top user of nuclear power that is not also a nuclear weapon state. The only states producing more nuclear power than the ROK (China, France, Russia, and the United States) all have nuclear weapons. Thus South Korea's rise to this position gives it a special standing and legitimacy in its commitment to nonproliferation. In many senses it serves as a poster child for the efficacy of the nuclear regimes that regulate nuclear energy and trade while seeking to prevent nuclear weapons proliferation. That these regimes were largely built by the weapon states to protect their own interests—and, some would argue, to perpetuate their technological dominance at the expense of developing countries—makes the ROK's emergence all the more interesting as an example of how a middle power can gain a position of prominence in the international system. This special standing in turn has yielded opportunities for South Korea to shape the regimes that govern its nuclear activities.

This position is still relatively new for the ROK, having coalesced in the 2009–2012 time frame. Before 2009, South Korea had been a participant in the nuclear regimes, but it rarely (if ever) sought leadership in nuclear diplomacy. Two events, which coincided with the Lee Myung-bak administration's Global Korea initiative, changed the ROK's nuclear diplomacy calculus. First, on May 25, 2009, North Korea (the Democratic People's Republic of Korea, or DPRK) conducted a second nuclear explosive test. South Korea's actions after the test demonstrate sharp movement away from its history of DPRK-centric nuclear diplomacy toward aggressive activities in international nuclear regimes. On May 26, the ROK joined the Proliferation Security Initiative—a counterproliferation mechanism whose members seek to interdict illicit trafficking of nuclear goods—and shortly thereafter elevated its involvement with another group, the Global Initiative to Combat Nuclear Terrorism. Second, in late December 2009, South Korea concluded a

$20 billion agreement to construct four nuclear power plants in the United Arab Emirates. This deal marked the ROK's emergence as a nuclear exporter and its aspirations for nuclear industry to become a major export sector alongside automobiles, electronics, and steel.

These two events catalyzed a broadening of Seoul's vision of its nuclear policy, planting the seeds of South Korea's interest to play more of a leadership role in international efforts to strengthen nuclear safety and security. Events after 2009 allowed these seeds to grow. North Korea's further provocations in 2010 (the sinking of the *Cheonan* and shelling of Yeonpyeong), the Fukushima nuclear accident in March 2011, and the initiation of U.S.-ROK negotiations on a renewal of their bilateral nuclear cooperation agreement elevated nuclear issues to the top of South Korea's national security and diplomacy priorities. Seoul's emerging leadership in nuclear regimes served multiple interests.

Those interests seemingly coalesced in the Lee administration's initiative to host the 2012 Nuclear Security Summit (NSS) in Seoul, which serves as this chapter's focus for examining South Korea's role as a middle power in international nuclear safety and security governance.

This chapter describes South Korea's rise to the international nuclear elite, how its interests and motivations evolved over time, and how this evolution set the stage for its hosting of the 2012 Nuclear Security Summit. Using that summit as case study of South Korea's middle power diplomacy, the chapter assesses the extent to which the ROK's substantive and procedural contributions affected the summit outcomes and reviews the domestic and international legacies of the summit now three years hence to evaluate the effectiveness of South Korea's leadership. This review suggests that although Korea marshaled significant diplomatic capacity and built a foundation for leadership on nuclear safety and security through the summit, since then institutional capacity for sustained involvement has fragmented, and a durable political commitment has been lacking, raising important questions about whether and how the ROK might continue to lead efforts to strengthen nuclear safety and security, both regionally and globally.

SOUTH KOREA'S RISE WITHIN THE NUCLEAR ORDER

South Korea's strategy for export-led economic growth—the basis for its rapid industrialization and development following the Korean

War—required significant energy inputs. Nuclear power provided the
ROK a major source of base-load electricity generation to fuel its industry, but just as it was for many developing states, nuclear technology was
also a potent symbol of modernity. South Korea initiated its nuclear
power program in the 1970s, based initially on technology imported from
the United States and other suppliers, but also clearly with a short-term
objective to become self-sufficient in nuclear energy to the extent possible. Indeed, as Figure 3 demonstrates, South Korea's nuclear electricity
growth curve is closely correlated with per capita GDP growth.

At first, South Korea imported turnkey systems, including its first
reactors, which were supplied by the United States for the Kori plant
and by Canada for the Wolsong plant. But as it gained experience in
constructing and operating nuclear power plants, the ROK began to
increase the domestic portions of subsequent reactor builds. Soon a
supply chain to manufacture many of the critical components for its
reactors was in place. Doosan Heavy Industries, in particular, began
to manufacture the large reactor pressure vessels and other major steel
elements of nuclear power plants, building on South Korea's emergence as a leading steel manufacturer. Today, Doosan is one of the few
companies in the world that maintains the large forges necessary to pro-
duce these critical reactor components, a reflection of South Korea's
successful efforts to indigenize production higher up the value chain
across many of its export sectors.

FIGURE 3. GDP PER CAPITA VS. NUCLEAR ELECTRICITY GROWTH

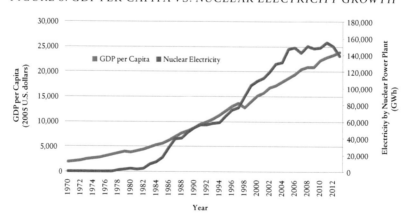

Sources: World Bank (GDP); Electric Power Statistics Information System (nuclear electricity), https://
epsis.kpx.or.kr/.

As the ROK's nuclear program took shape with international assistance in the late 1970s, so too did its involvement with the nonproliferation regime. South Korea joined the International Atomic Energy Agency (IAEA) in 1957 and signed the Nuclear Nonproliferation Treaty in 1968. Given its technological reliance on foreign nuclear suppliers, South Korea's adherence to the nonproliferation regime presumably was seen as an important enabler of nuclear cooperation. Yet membership in the regimes did not stop the administration of President Park Chung-hee from considering development of nuclear weapons in the mid-1970s. However, following heavy pressure from the administration of U.S. President Jimmy Carter, including threats to block nuclear cooperation and withdraw U.S. troops from ROK territory, Park terminated the nascent nuclear weapons effort. Since then, with the exception of two safeguards violations for failing to report to the IAEA experiments involving plutonium separation and uranium enrichment, South Korea's nonproliferation record has been clean.

As South Korea's nuclear energy generation increased during the 1980s, its ability to supply nuclear components, first to its own industry and then to foreign markets, also grew. Recognizing the ROK's growing importance as a potential supplier and the commensurate desire that it adhere to international export control standards, the Nuclear Suppliers Group (NSG) invited South Korea to become a participating government in 1996. Foreshadowing its later use of "host diplomacy," South Korea served as chair of the NSG in 2003 and hosted the group's annual plenary meeting that year in Busan.[1]

Even though South Korean involvement with international regimes increased as its nuclear power program grew, its rise within the nuclear order was (and remains) constrained by two important bilateral agreements. First, under the terms of the U.S.-ROK nuclear cooperation agreement signed in 1972, South Korea is not permitted to develop more sensitive, advanced nuclear capabilities, in particular for reprocessing of U.S.-origin nuclear fuel.[2] Second, in a 1992 joint declaration with North Korea, the ROK agreed not to build either plutonium reprocessing or uranium enrichment capabilities. Although these technologies can be used in peaceful nuclear power programs, they also can yield fissile materials that are the core ingredients of nuclear weapons. Both agreements blocked South Korea's development of these technologies on nonproliferation grounds, but in the process also created impediments (both real and perceived) to its leadership standing within the regime.

Notwithstanding these constraints, nuclear energy continued to grow in importance in the ROK into the 2000s, with ever-increasing projections of the number of units to be built and the share of electricity generation served by nuclear. As of early 2015, South Korea generated more than 14 gigawatts electrical (GWe) from nuclear power, equaling about 30 percent of its total electricity production.[3] Given South Korea's near total dependence on imported energy, nuclear power represents a critical component of the country's energy security strategy. This dependence also gives South Korea a strong domestic interest in expanding its role in international nuclear governance regimes, but the ability of middle powers such as the ROK to assert leadership in such regimes remains uncertain.

EVOLVING INTERESTS, GROWING ASPIRATIONS

As South Korea's technical prowess in building and operating nuclear power plants grew, so too did its intention to become a technology provider rather than merely an importer. First, in the 1990s, nuclear physicists and engineers at the Korea Electric Power Company (KEPCO) and the Korea Atomic Energy Research Institute (KAERI) worked to develop a standardized design for a 1,000-megawatt electrical power plant (later designated the Optimized Power Reactor). South Korea subsequently built ten plants from these designs and began to market them for export to developing countries in Asia, particularly Indonesia and Vietnam.[4] But by the late 1990s, South Korea had begun to develop interests in more advanced nuclear capabilities, in particular a form of reprocessing called pyroprocessing. South Korean scientists also began to explore the potential for a second-stage nuclear fuel cycle based on fast neutron reactors.

Sensing opportunities to advance its own nuclear research agenda, as well as its standing with nuclear nations, in the early 2000s the ROK joined two international nuclear research arrangements: the Generation IV International Forum and the International Project on Innovative Nuclear Reactors and Fuel Cycles. Such collaboration served to boost interest in advanced nuclear research programs in South Korea, but more important, it gave South Korean scientists regular opportunities to interact with peers from the major nuclear states. By joining these initiatives, the ROK began to be perceived as an advanced nuclear state, joining the likes of the United States, France, Russia, and Japan.[5] And

South Korean officials and scientists also began to see themselves as part of the nuclear elite, which provided both confidence and impetus to demonstrate leadership in the field.

South Korea's growing aspirations for the nuclear sciences coincided with a push by the government to develop nuclear energy as a new export sector. Over the course of several national plans for energy development starting in 2007, the South Korean government affirmed plans to develop a larger advanced reactor (the APR-1400); to become a global top-five nuclear energy producer, including a goal to generate up to 60 percent of electricity using nuclear power; and to become the third-largest exporter of nuclear reactors, capturing 20 percent of the global market by 2030.[6] After the December 2009 announcement of the $20 billion sale of four APR-1400s to the United Arab Emirates, South Korea seemed well on its way to reaching these targets and becoming what might be termed a major nuclear energy power.[7]

The domestic motivations and sense of growth potential in 2009 for South Korea in this area, however, ran up against two challenges that came to a head during the Lee administration (2008–2013). First, despite its advanced nuclear science and industry, South Korea was unable to convince the United States, during negotiations on a new bilateral nuclear cooperation agreement, to consent to the ROK's development of fuel cycle capabilities, in particular the pyroprocessing technology sought by KAERI. For Washington, this issue was seen primarily as a nonproliferation matter, but many South Korean experts and commentators felt that U.S. policy was not fair and was blocking the ROK's nuclear development potential.

Second, South Korea's nuclear diplomacy is in many ways inseparable from international concerns about North Korea's nuclear program. This linking of civil nuclear and nuclear weapons issues on the Korean peninsula partly explains Washington's opposition to ROK development of pyroprocessing, but it also seriously complicates Seoul's calculations about how to balance the nuclear elements of its foreign and national security policies. A series of DPRK provocations in 2009 and 2010 put this problem in sharp relief. On one level, it was precisely these provocations that set the stage for South Korea to first draw closer to and then seek leadership opportunities in international nuclear security regimes. On another level, however, South Korea's capacity and potential for leadership in such regimes is constrained by the predominance of the North Korea issue over all others in its policymaking. Put another way, any South Korean initiative to strengthen nuclear safety and security regimes will be viewed domestically for its implications and potential impact on efforts to denuclearize North Korea, rather than for its potential to advance international norms and practices and South Korea's standing as a major nuclear energy power. As will become clear in the following discussion, unless and until South Korea's nuclear energy program is fully separated from the question of North Korea's nuclear weapons program, it will be difficult for the ROK to develop and sustain the institutional capacity for global leadership on nuclear issues, and to become a norm setter rather than a norm follower.

THE 2012 SEOUL NUCLEAR SECURITY SUMMIT

In a nuclear-themed address in Prague in April 2009, U.S. President Barack Obama announced that he would convene a global summit on nuclear security, focused on preventing terrorists from accessing vulnerable nuclear material. President Lee was among the 47 heads of state and government who gathered at the inaugural summit in Washington, DC, in April 2010. At the talks' conclusion, Obama announced that South Korea would host the second nuclear security summit in 2012.

There are many reasons why Korea was an attractive NSS host from the U.S. point of view: it is a nonnuclear weapon state that would bring geographic diversity and Asian leadership to the gathering; it had recently joined the Proliferation Security Initiative and volunteered to host a Global Initiative to Combat Nuclear Terrorism leadership meeting; and it is a close U.S. ally, which would facilitate cooperation with Washington on process and substance in the lead-up to the summit. But from Seoul's point of view, why might South Korea seek to play a leadership role in the NSS, an initiative seeded and shaped by the United States and focused primarily on the security of fissile materials, which South Korea does not possess?

The answer to this question is not entirely clear, even in hindsight. Apart from the surface similarity of the 2012 NSS and the 2010 G20 summit, both of which were keystones of the Lee administration's Global Korea policy and so-called host diplomacy, it seems that at least some of the ROK's nuclear policy priorities between 2010 and 2012 were in tension with, or were at least not aided by, its hosting of the NSS. In particular, there was significant confusion about the objectives of the summit and how it would advance the ROK's interests. Based on a review of South Korean diplomacy during this period, and without asserting any order of priority, these interests were sixfold:

- To strengthen nuclear safety and security regimes given their intrinsic importance to advanced nuclear states.
- To maintain domestic consensus on nuclear power by building public confidence for advanced nuclear operations in light of South Korea's energy security challenge and limited energy supply options.
- To open up international markets for ROK nuclear exports, focusing in particular on Southeast Asia.
- To burnish South Korea's reputation on the global stage and demonstrate nonproliferation bona fides.
- To spur diplomatic efforts to resolve the DPRK nuclear issue while denying Pyongyang space for its own diplomacy and efforts to legitimize its nuclear weapons.
- To make progress on negotiations toward a new nuclear cooperation agreement with the United States that would facilitate ROK development of fuel cycle capabilities as a potential option for handling South Korea's spent fuel accumulation problem.

Of these interests, hosting the NSS was most consonant with the first, fourth, and potentially the sixth. (Regarding the sixth, in interviews at the time, several U.S. and ROK officials rejected any overt connection between South Korea's offer to host the NSS and its ambitions in nuclear cooperation negotiations with the United States, but the perception of a connection is understandable.) Indeed, hosting the NSS raised awkward questions, in particular about whether and how the ROK could use the summit to advance its DPRK policy, while a focus on threats to nuclear security is not particularly helpful for maintaining domestic support for nuclear power nor for marketing reactors to potential foreign clients.

The tension with DPRK policy, which is the most central nuclear priority in South Korea's national security policy, posed the most enduring challenge to the Lee administration's handling of the NSS. The South Korean public, media, and even some foreign policy experts seemed to expect that Seoul could leverage the summit to highlight North Korean intransigence and promote norms that would pressure Pyongyang to denuclearize.[8] The link between the two issues was inadvertently boosted by Lee himself, who issued a public invitation to North Korea to join the summit, but only if it first agreed to denuclearize and return to the Six Party Talks.[9] This linkage dogged the summit preparation process and carried through the gathering itself, where South Korean and international media continued to speculate how the parties would address North Korea's nuclear activities.[10] Although certain leaders participating in the summit did issue side statements denouncing North Korea's nuclear weapons, and Lee reportedly raised North Korea in his bilateral meetings with other leaders, South Korea's hosting of the summit ultimately seems to have had no bearing on diplomacy with the North—at least, there is no evidence to suggest that any subsequent diplomatic initiatives with North Korea are tied to the summit in any way.

ASSESSING ROK SUMMIT DIPLOMACY

Despite the assessment that hosting the NSS had little bearing on several of South Korea's nuclear priorities, and setting aside the reputational benefit, was South Korea able to put its stamp on the process and outcomes of the summit itself in ways that demonstrated a role for middle-power diplomacy? Available evidence, detailed in this section, suggests that the ROK was able to achieve some modest successes in its diplomacy, to capitalize on the opportunity of hosting the summit, and to demonstrate that it had standing and legitimacy in a policy area that tends to be dominated by major powers. That said, South Korea also encountered some challenges and limitations in its ability to set the agenda for the summit and bridge disparate perspectives.

It is notable that South Korea mobilized significant internal resources, largely based on human-resource capacity, in order to implement a successful summit. It placed two seasoned diplomats in charge of the external diplomacy and negotiation of the summit communiqué, it established a preparatory interagency committee chaired by the prime minister and a standing secretariat led by the foreign minister, and it mounted a major public diplomacy campaign for participating states and the Korean public.[11] It also facilitated in parallel to the main summit an expert symposium and nuclear industry summit. As will be discussed further, this mobilization has had some lasting domestic impact on nuclear policy in Korea. The investment of resources and careful preparation not only ensured a successful summit; it also guaranteed that South Korea would continue to be viewed as a leader of the nuclear security enterprise well after the Seoul summit concluded.

In the lead-up to the summit, the ROK championed several substantive priorities that it sought to place on the agenda. Several of these priorities were perceived to be contrary to U.S. interests, and some South Korean analysts have argued that Seoul's successful efforts to raise them demonstrate effective leadership of the summit process and independence from the United States.[12] In particular, South Korea sought to broaden the discussion of threat beyond fissile materials that can be used in nuclear weapons to include radioactive sources that are ubiquitous in industrialized countries and whose theft and use by terrorists poses a more likely if less devastating threat than the potential terrorist use of nuclear weapons. Additionally, in light of the March 2011 Fukushima nuclear accident in Japan, South Korea supported discussion of a "nuclear safety-security nexus" during the summit. Inclusion of both issues on the agenda necessarily diluted the narrow focus on fissile material security, which is how the summit process had been initially framed and promoted by the United States. Without access to official records, it is difficult to assess the extent to which U.S.-ROK tension over these issues was more perceived than real, as well as how instrumental South Korean diplomacy was in negotiations over the agenda and summit communiqué. Secondary sources (albeit mainly from the United States, not the ROK) and background interviews, coupled with a nuanced reading of the communiqués, do yield some tentative findings.

First, South Korean diplomats did manage to build international consensus on the inclusion of radiological source security on the agenda, but the evidence suggests this was less a matter of South Korean agenda-setting than deft diplomacy. A comparison of the Washington and Seoul summit communiqués is instructive in this regard. The 2010 Washington communiqué, closely reflecting U.S. framing of the issues, mentions radioactive source security in only one instance and asserts that mere acknowledgement, rather than development and implementation, of steps to promote nuclear security would improve the security of radioactive sources. The 2012 communiqué, in comparison, mentions radioactive source security fifteen times, including in a dedicated paragraph.[13] This is a significant broadening of the agenda beyond Washington's preferred focus. But according to secondary source reports, it was Germany, not South Korea, that led the charge on including radioactive source security in the agenda.[14] In this sense, South Korean diplomats demonstrated adroit diplomacy to manage divergent views between the founder (the United States) and other states with different priorities. South Korea further showed creative thinking in announcing a partnership with Vietnam and the IAEA to develop a radioactive source tracking system that would be piloted by Vietnam. This showed a commitment beyond diplomacy to exercise of leadership in the region, a role the ROK might usefully expand in the future.

Second, on the inclusion of nuclear safety in the summit agenda, it seems inconceivable that the Seoul summit, which was held in Asia just over a year after the Fukushima accident, would not have addressed nuclear safety in some way. ROK officials may have sought a more expansive nuclear safety discussion than the United States was prepared to support, but gaining consensus on even the narrower formulation of the safety-security nexus was not a foregone conclusion, and several states apparently objected that nuclear safety was properly in the domain of other institutions and forums.[15] Ultimately, South Korean negotiators (with U.S. support) succeeded in scheduling a lunch during the summit to discuss the issue and in securing consensus of the participating governments on language in the communiqué, calling on states to design and implement nuclear safety and security measures "in a coherent and synergistic manner." This fairly anodyne language indicates a minor diplomatic victory, but one that set the stage for more progressive thinking. Indeed, at the 2014 Hague Nuclear Security Summit, participating states not only reaffirmed the need for coherent management of both safety and security, but also stipulated that states need to develop a nuclear security culture focused on the coordination of safety and security and seek continuous improvement in both areas.

Aside from these substantive efforts to shape the agenda to reflect the broader interests of the majority of participating states, South Korean experts also highlight two procedural successes of Seoul's summit leadership. The first purported success was "the transformation from an American-led initiative to a more universal-based normative one," one that is more reflective of global concerns and not "excessively dominated by U.S. interests."[16] However, this assertion seems at odds with the fact that all of the sherpa and sous-sherpa meetings were co-chaired by South Korean and U.S. officials, who cooperated extensively on the meeting agendas and communiqué drafts.[17] Describing the high level of cooperation between the two states on summit preparation, one U.S. official asserted that "the United States was the hand in the Korean glove."[18] This is not indicative of a process shorn of U.S. interest.

The second procedural success highlighted by South Korean experts was the expansion of participation from 47 to 53 states, indicative of the ROK's "middle power diplomacy tactics" and "bridging role" between established, emerging, and nonaligned powers.[19] Yet the six additional states that joined the summit—Azerbaijan, Denmark, Gabon, Hungary, Lithuania, and Romania—are not particularly compelling cases of "bridging," for none of them are ideational leaders of the nonaligned movement (as opposed to, say, Cuba), nor are any true emerging economies. A more compelling case of bridging and transformation of the U.S.-led initiative would have been if South Korea had secured the participation of a state such as Venezuela, which is among the leading voices of the nonaligned movement, or Niger, which is a large uranium supplier, but neither of these states participated in the Seoul summit.

At least one other procedural issue that arose during the negotiation of the communiqué demonstrated the limitations of Korea's middle-power diplomacy. According to some summit participants, negotiations became bogged down when it came to the responsibility of states with nuclear weapons to take extra precautions to secure fissile material in weaponized form. India and Pakistan, in particular, apparently objected to any mention of the security of nuclear weapons. South Korean diplomats were unable to negotiate language that satisfied these states. In the end, it was the U.S. team that brokered compromise language, which was incorporated into the perambulatory element of the 2012 communiqué. Given the sensitivities of this issue, as well as the special responsibilities of states possessing nuclear weapons, it is not surprising that a viable option had to originate from another nuclear weapon state, suggesting some limitations in the ability of nonnuclear weapon states (and middle powers) such as South Korea to perform agenda setting and bargaining functions on hard security issues.

LEGACY OF THE SEOUL SUMMIT

An accurate assessment of the significance of an event such as the 2012 NSS requires some remove. Now, three years after the summit, it is possible to identify several domestic and international legacies that further highlight the possibilities and limitations of South Korea's nuclear safety and security leadership efforts.

First, in terms of the development of expertise in South Korea and its capacity for leadership, the summit's achievements have been significant and, as yet, sustained. At the Washington summit, the ROK committed to establishing a nuclear security center of excellence, which now performs training for both domestic and international nuclear specialists. Some South Korean experts suggest this center has resulted in improved safety and security awareness at South Korean nuclear facilities. The Korea Institute of Nuclear Accounting and Control is charged with operating the center, and as a result its policy and technical expertise have grown along with its budget. There is also seemingly greater awareness of and interest in nuclear safety and security issues, indicated by the establishment of an informal nuclear policy society among technical and policy experts in Seoul.[20]

Yet the domestic outcomes also reveal gaps in Seoul's capacity to lead with credibility. For example, the recent scandal involving faked safety certificates for parts installed in South Korean nuclear reactors highlights the need for more attention to cultivating a nuclear safety and security culture in the ROK that improves practices at home while bolstering its reputation abroad.[21] South Korea's recently established regulatory organization—the Nuclear Safety and Security Commission—still lacks expertise, which undermines its independence and ability to lead a process to correct the regulatory deficiencies that contributed to the falsified certificates scandal. (Lack of effective government oversight of industry is an endemic problem in South Korea that affects numerous sectors, not just nuclear; the *Sewol* ferry disaster in April 2014 occurred largely because of regulatory capture by the shipping industry.) Effective leadership on nuclear safety and security on the international stage does not require perfection at home; however, it does require an ability to identify gaps and to address them critically, transparently, and with sustained commitment.

It is also worth noting here another prerequisite of sustained international leadership: capable diplomacy backed by an interagency support network at home. As described earlier, South Korea mobilized a major intergovernmental effort to host the summit, but since then both its diplomatic capacity and interagency process to support global leadership on nuclear safety and security appear to have withered. The multiple interagency groups formed to support the summit were not institutionalized, and they dissolved following the summit's conclusion. Many of the diplomats and technical specialists who worked on the summit have moved on to other issues, and there has been no dedicated effort to develop technical or policy expertise within the foreign ministry or other agencies. To be sure, South Korea has talented nuclear engineers and scientists, as well as capable diplomats, but global leadership also requires policy entrepreneurs and innovators who understand both policy and technology and who can blend them in creative ways. A return to normal governmental operations is to be expected after hosting a major meeting, but as one of only three governments to have hosted an NSS (the United States and the Netherlands complete the leadership troika), South Korea's ability to sustain leadership is threatened by this diminution of capacity.

Perhaps more troubling is that the administration of President Park Geun-hye appears to have concluded that the 2012 summit is a legacy of the previous Lee administration, rather than an opportunity for continued leadership. Instead, Park has pursued her own nuclear initiatives (including one focused on regional nuclear safety) that appear to have neither international traction nor the type of internal support structure borne by a political commitment such as the NSS. Without durable political commitments and sustained institutional capacity, it will be a challenge for South Korea to maintain leadership of any issue, including nuclear safety and security, on the international stage.

Assessing the international legacy of the 2012 Seoul summit is somewhat more difficult. As part of the NSS troika, South Korea continues to be perceived as a leader of this effort along with the United States. Several ongoing activities demonstrate South Korea's leadership intentions: a regional initiative formed with Japan and China to coordinate the work of their respective nuclear centers of excellence; the ROK's sharing of technical knowledge to develop high-density reactor fuels that would facilitate conversion of research reactors for use with safer, low-enriched uranium; and cosponsoring an initiative with the Netherlands and the United States during the 2014 NSS to strengthen nuclear security implementation. South Korea reportedly is preparing an initiative on cybersecurity for nuclear facilities for the 2016 summit. Along with the maturation of issues it seeded during the 2012 summit (for instance, on the nuclear safety-security nexus), these activities demonstrate continued substantive commitment to joint leadership of the NSS process.

But with the shifting nature of the nuclear security agenda and the decision by the participating governments to conclude the summit process in 2016, it remains to be seen whether and how South Korea can continue to exercise middle-power leadership on nuclear safety and security in the future. This same question hangs over the United States, for the NSS process was an Obama administration legacy, and it is uncertain whether his successor will maintain a strong commitment to the issue. Given that South Korea's leadership in this endeavor was facilitated by the United States having established the process—placing South Korea in more of a bandwagoning role—it seems that fading U.S. interest might also diminish continued opportunities for South Korea's nuclear diplomacy. Then again, fading U.S. commitment to the issue might open new opportunities for the ROK to fill a leadership vacuum. South Korea now has some pedigree, domestic resources, and the international standing to build on its efforts to strengthen nuclear safety and security both regionally and globally. Yet the promise of such a role will remain unfulfilled until South Korea develops a cadre of experts and there is a sustained political commitment to exercising leadership on these issues beyond host diplomacy. This is not merely criticism from an outside observer, but a point made also by South Korean experts critical of the government's lack of follow-through. Writing after the Seoul summit, Shin Chang-Hoon argued that South Koreans "need to reflect on whether we were simply interested in hosting the event or we were seriously interested in achieving nuclear security and taking leadership."[22]

CONCLUSIONS

For South Korea, hosting the 2012 Nuclear Security Summit did not result in any breakthroughs in nuclear diplomacy with North Korea. It did not contribute to South Korea's aspirations to sell more nuclear power reactors overseas nor materially change the terms of the U.S.-ROK nuclear cooperation agreement negotiations in ways favorable to South Korea. All of these issues had their own dynamics outside of the NSS process, and despite misplaced hopes by some South Korean foreign policy experts and the broader public, there were at best marginal opportunities for South Korea to advance these interests using the NSS platform. Yet South Korea certainly burnished its reputation as a leading nuclear power with its aspirations to set the norm on nuclear safety and security. It marshaled significant resources and made substantive and procedural contributions to the summit in ways that broadened the global basis of the effort, though they were in concert with U.S. ideals.

In seizing the opportunity to host the summit, South Korea built a platform from which to exert influence in the future.

And yet, as described here, South Korea's efforts during and actions subsequent to the 2012 summit—in particular the perception of diminished capacity and interest in these issues under the Park administration—calls into question its desire and ability to exercise effective leadership in the future. The gains from 2012 will be ephemeral unless the ROK seizes the opportunity of the final summit in 2016 to cement its role as a leading implementer of nuclear security in Asia and global agenda-setter working hand in hand with the United States, the Netherlands, and others to transition the NSS process to a durable global nuclear security architecture. South Korea may play a unique role if it chooses, for it possesses comparative advantages in technological resources and regional positioning. It can utilize its center of excellence to train a world-class cadre of nuclear technology and policy specialists to help staff the IAEA and other institutions that will be pillars of the global nuclear security architecture. Seoul can invest more in training and related efforts to strengthen nuclear security practices among developing states in Asia, even as it builds its domestic pool of experts. And it can seek a more active bridging role by working with states that for political reasons are unlikely to seek help from the United States, Russia, China, or others for nuclear safety and security assistance. But to fulfill this leadership potential, South Korea should work harder to maintain both the technical and policy expertise developed around the 2012 summit, and to build institutions within the government to sustain the political commitment made by President Lee.

South Korea's Role as Host of the Green Climate Fund: Implications for ROK Contributions to Green Growth

Jill Kosch O'Donnell

In October 2012, four months before the end of South Korean President Lee Myung-bak's term, the board of the new Green Climate Fund (GCF) announced the selection of Songdo, South Korea, as its host city. This was a major win for Lee; it capped a five-year term in office that was marked by an aggressive push at home and abroad for low-carbon green growth, a strategy that aims to reduce greenhouse gas emissions while developing new drivers of economic growth through investments in clean-energy technologies. Lee's efforts were timely; UN-led global climate negotiations are currently coalescing around the idea that developing countries—especially highly advanced ones such as South Korea—should do more to address climate change even though the United Nations Framework Convention on Climate Change (UNFCCC) does not require them to do so. Developing countries now account for more than half of global greenhouse gas emissions.[1] Many of them are demanding help in adapting to climate change effects and in seeking plans that can shift their economies away from reliance on carbon sources without sacrificing growth. These dynamics have given rise to increasing interest in whether green growth actually works. The linchpin is money, and the GCF's role is crucial in that regard. It was created through UN climate negotiations to channel investment to climate change mitigation and adaptation projects in developing countries. This mission is now closely linked with efforts to reach a climate deal in Paris in 2015 to succeed the Kyoto Protocol, which expires in 2020.

Lee's efforts left South Korea in a stronger position to lead on green growth. There is no question that he succeeded in establishing a set of laws, institutions, and expectations that no Blue House successor could easily dismiss. In 2009, his administration announced a voluntary greenhouse gas reduction target of 30 percent below the 2020 expected level, creating a pledge that his successor would have to address. Under his watch, South Korea set a double precedent, becoming the first developing country and the first in Asia to approve a nationwide emissions trading scheme. The launch of the Seoul-based Global Green Growth Institute as an international organization in 2012 has helped secure a long-term role for an ROK-inspired organization on a topic of growing global interest. Finally, as host of the GCF, South Korea is home to an organization whose efforts are central to two factors that will define global climate negotiations for the foreseeable future: promoting developing country participation and climate finance. This groundwork paved the way for future South Korean leadership on green growth, but it cannot sustain itself. Whether it can translate into continued South Korean influence depends on national leadership committed to the pursuit of green growth and ready to capitalize on the diplomatic openings Lee created.

POSITIONING SOUTH KOREA FOR A NEW CLIMATE LANDSCAPE

When Lee took office in 2008, a convergence of interests and opportunity presented a ripe moment for the launch of his signature policy, low-carbon green growth. On the international front, countries were beginning to negotiate a successor to the Kyoto Protocol, and discussions about what developing countries might do to reduce greenhouse gas emissions were already occurring.[2] Lee's election in December 2007 came just days after the thirteenth round of UN climate negotiations in Bali, Indonesia, which produced an expectation that developing countries should do something to rein in greenhouse gas emissions.[3]

The 1992 UNFCCC designated developed countries as "Annex I" countries, which have legally binding emissions reduction commitments; all other countries at the time (including South Korea) were considered "non–Annex I" developing countries with no such legally binding commitments. Certainly by the time Lee took office, this blunt division of countries into two categories did not reflect almost twenty years' worth of major changes in economic growth rates and emissions levels. South Korea's rapid economic growth, ascension to membership in the OECD in 1996, and designation as the OECD's fastest-growing source of greenhouse gas emissions between 1990 and 2005 made clear that a UN framework that included South Korea and Haiti in the same category was no longer relevant. Indeed, in a 2008 OECD paper that proposes new categories for differentiating countries under the UNFCCC, South Korea was included in seven out of eight definitions of developed countries.[4] The country appeared to be headed toward a future of climate obligations; pursuing a policy of low-carbon green growth was a way to take charge of this fate, preempting a measure of international pressure and earning plaudits along the way for taking action. Subsequent developments bore this out; UN-sponsored negotiations since that time have sought to clarify expectations for all countries to take steps to limit greenhouse gas emissions.

At home, the ROK's near-total reliance on imports to meet its energy needs was an important concern. The desire to increase energy independence and boost economic growth were major drivers of green growth, which Lee called a new "national development paradigm" that regarded environmental protection and economic growth as compatible and even mutually reinforcing. Under Lee, green growth was aimed at reducing greenhouse gas emissions, creating new engines of economic growth through investments in clean energy technologies, and enhancing South Korea's role on the international stage.

Arguably, Lee's green growth policies were more successful in positioning the ROK to play a greater global role in contributing to knowledge development of green growth than they were in achieving concrete domestic benefits. The 2014 Global Green Economy Index ranked South Korea much higher on perceptions of green growth policies (twenty-third out of sixty) than on performance (thirty-ninth out of sixty), citing the "relative carbon inefficiency of its economy and surprisingly poor environmental performance."[5] This finding makes sense in light of Lee's ambitious policies, which drew praise from across the globe but have yet to result in real benefits.[6] For example, the emissions trading scheme (ETS) took effect in January 2015, though continued pushback from industry groups has weakened its design.[7] South Korea's greenhouse gas emissions continue to grow, calling into question whether the country will meet its voluntary emissions reduction target.[8]

The Global Green Economy Index gave South Korea high marks in the markets-and-investment category, which measures countries' attractiveness in renewable energy investment as well as clean technology innovation and government support for green investment. In line with this finding, South Korea ranked eleventh on Ernst and Young's most recent

Renewable Energy Country Attractiveness Index, unchanged from its previous ranking and scoring eleventh or better in the solar photovoltaic, biomass, and marine energy categories.[9] The Lee administration's push for a smart-grid pilot project on Jeju Island recently led to Korea Electric Power Company's first deal to export smart-grid technology in October 2014.[10] These results seem consistent with Lee's characterization of green growth as a source of new growth engines, an idea that current President Park Geun-hye continues to emphasize under the policy approach she has dubbed "creative economy." Despite this investment environment, the amount of renewable energy in the ROK's energy mix remains small, standing at less than 3 percent as of 2012.[11]

Lee was an early and enthusiastic promoter of green growth, helping to propel it into the global conversation. The phrase was a fixture in his public remarks throughout his time in office and a notable component of his diplomacy; he signed numerous memoranda of understanding for bilateral cooperation on green growth, which was not a widely used phrase before 2008. The OECD issued a green growth declaration for the first time in June 2009, and entirely new institutions have since sprung up around the concept, including the Green Growth Knowledge Platform, the Climate Development Knowledge Network, and the Green Growth Best Practice Initiative.

The discussion surrounding green growth today is replete with references to the idea that it is still a work in progress. Conferences and reports include topics such as "Towards a Definition of Green Growth," and "What Is Inclusive Green Growth?"[12] A survey conducted as part of the 2014 Global Green Economy Index found that there is a "high level of uncertainty surrounding the definition of 'green economy' across geographies, sectors, and particularly between different types of organizations and institutions."[13] Beyond definitional differences, the current literature on green growth seems to agree on two crucial points: there is no one-size-fits-all approach to green growth, and it is too soon to judge which strategies can be effective.[14] If green growth is to ever take hold on a scale that can drive transformational change, the world will need proof that it works. This is precisely what Lee created the Global Green Growth Institute (GGGI) to do. The GGGI is an important reflection of South Korea's middle-power identity and capacity on green growth and a significant potential source of the country's long-term contributions to it.

"ME FIRST" AND MIDDLE POWER

President Lee often described his green growth policies as a "me first" strategy, referring to the idea that countries should act on climate change mitigation without waiting for other countries to act first.[15] The voluntary emissions reduction target was a major component of this strategy. But two questions remained: What could South Korea really achieve by "going first"? And if the country did decide to go first, would anyone follow?

These questions point toward the ROK's middle-power identity and capacity. The issue of climate change and the burgeoning concept of green growth, combined with twenty years of little success in UN-sponsored climate negotiations, invite middle-power leadership, especially of a South Korean brand. There are at least two reasons for this. First, Lee arrived in office at a time when it was becoming clear that new approaches were needed beyond haggling over emissions targets and timetables and that developing countries would be expected to play a larger role in the future. This was an opportune time for a middle power to show that it could forge ahead. To be sure, the math on global emissions shows that they cannot be reined in without action from the United States and China.[16] They are the world's two largest emitters, together accounting for more than one-third of global greenhouse gas emissions.[17] South Korea, which contributes 1.8 percent of global carbon dioxide emissions, is too small to make a difference alone.[18] But setting a voluntary emissions reduction target, as Lee did, could send a message to other countries whose participation is needed.

The limits and opportunities of South Korea's middle-power status are clear in this case: the country's rapid emissions growth due to its fast development means that it can command some attention for this action, but not enough to make a material difference. The significance lies in the potential to build a bridge, however tenuous, over the developed/developing country divide by voluntarily doing more. South Korea is both a non–Annex I country and a member of the OECD. The country has recent memories of rapid development yet experiences the same type of industry opposition to emissions trading that the United States does. Even though going first did not initiate a wave of voluntary commitments from other developing countries, it did gain the country some attention. If South Korea can deliver on its emissions reduction target and demonstrate real substance behind the green growth slogan, then there may be lessons for both developed and developing counties to draw on.

Second, if, as scholars such as Sook-Jong Lee assert, one important attribute of a middle power is the pursuit of policy leadership in niche areas where it has a strong interest or advantage, then green growth is a natural fit for a middle power such as South Korea.[19] The country's advantage in green growth stems from two factors. First, the need to diversify energy sources in a country that is almost totally reliant on imports creates deep motivation to do so in new and creative ways. The fact that South Korea is pursuing oil and gas deals around the globe simultaneously with green growth can be read as pragmatic or inconsistent; this really illustrates that global knowledge of green growth's possibilities and limitations is still young and limited but growing. Second, growing pressure on developing countries to do more to mitigate climate change has created some demand for proof that green growth actually works and a willingness to accept assistance in trying. In 2012, South Korea pledged to increase the amount of its green official development assistance to 30 percent of total ODA by 2020.[20] The Korea International Cooperation Agency currently has plans under way ranging from renewable energy projects in Cameroon to green-city master plan development in Vietnam.[21] In addition, with its own experience as a fast developer and the benefit of decades of lessons learned in international development practices that have come to emphasize the importance of local ownership, South Korea has stepped into a leadership role on this issue by creating the GGGI. The GGGI's approach can resonate with developing countries because it emphasizes the importance of economic growth as a first principle, as illustrated by this stark admission in its most recent strategic plan: "There has been no poverty reduction at scale without strong economic growth."[22] By working in-country on tailored plans for green growth that align with national development priorities, the GGGI aims to prove that green growth is possible and to share best practices developed over time through direct experience. The organization is new and small—it has a proposed 2015 core budget of only $29.7 million.[23] But an international policy agenda crowded with a diverse range of issues means there is an opportunity for a middle power to step up on a specific task such as proving green growth.

As an international organization, the GGGI is no longer wholly "Korean," but its creation represents a major diplomatic success for the

ROK; the Lee administration conceived of the idea and made it reality. This required securing the financial, diplomatic, and intellectual support of other countries to try something new: a hands-on approach to green growth inspired by South Korea's own development experiences. A strong relationship between the South Korean government and the GGGI will remain mutually beneficial to both parties. The government can be a champion for its homegrown institution and provide diplomatic support for its future expansion efforts. The GGGI and the South Korean government can also partner on pushing the green growth agenda globally.

PRESIDENT PARK'S PARADIGM: IT'S ALL ABOUT THE (BUSINESS) ENVIRONMENT

Although low-carbon green growth played a starring role in President Lee's policy agenda, it occupies a more peripheral position under President Park's "creative economy" rubric. Overall, Park is firmly focused on boosting economic growth.[24] In public remarks, she has tended to highlight climate change as an economic opportunity, emphasizing investment in new energy industries to "ignite fresh engines of future growth."[25] Her creative economy entails a bottom-up approach that seeks to facilitate entrepreneurship. Under this formulation, climate change is only one of many challenges that the creative economy could address. In a 2014 speech to the World Economic Forum, Park described the creative economy as one that "harnesses the creative ideas of individuals and marries them with science and technology—with IT."[26] Her plan calls for the establishment of Centers for Creative Economy and Innovation in seventeen cities throughout all eight provinces to support start-ups; three had been established by the end of 2014.[27] She has also spoken about plans to create "environment-friendly towns" as pilot projects that generate electricity through new and renewable sources and then eventually "help them spread throughout the nation through voluntary participation."[28] However, the low-scale and voluntary nature of these plans may be far too little to advance low-carbon green growth as Lee articulated it.

Though Park has distanced herself from Lee's green growth agenda, South Korea's credibility on green growth will depend in large part on two policies she inherited from Lee: the emissions trading scheme and the voluntary emissions reduction target. Park has acknowledged the emissions reduction pledge as a "promise to the international community."[29] However, at least three factors constrain her ability to keep that promise. First, her administration has lowered the target for nuclear energy generation amid safety concerns following high-profile scandals at South Korean nuclear plants in 2013.[30] As an energy source that emits no greenhouse gases, nuclear power expansion was an important component of reducing future emissions in Lee's green growth strategy, and rebuilding its record in the eyes of the South Korean public is vital for continuing its expansion. Second, experts acknowledge the importance of reforming electricity prices, kept artificially low by the government, in order to reduce demand enough to help rein in emissions.[31] Raising these prices would likely be politically difficult. Finally, the ETS, which was intended as an instrument to help meet the target, has been weakened under the Park administration amid continued industry opposition.[32]

It is important to note that Lee, and any successor to him, would have faced these same external pressures on green growth goals and might have taken similar actions. Public opinion in South Korea suggests that Park may face difficult choices in balancing environmental and economic goals. In a 2014 poll, 77 percent of respondents agreed that climate change is caused by humans, but only 20 percent rated the ROK's economic situation as "good."[33] Lee set ambitious green growth goals and created a framework to advance them. But the hard work was bound to continue for any successive leader facing domestic politics and economic growth imperatives.

The international front may offer another avenue for continued South Korean leadership on green growth. First, Lee's green growth diplomacy may have created new opportunities for Park to exercise leadership. Hosting the GCF gives Park, and any future South Korean president, a platform for leading the dialogue on climate finance that she likely would not otherwise have. For example, Park chaired the side event on climate finance during the 2014 UN climate summit in New York. If Lee had not helped to secure Songdo as home to the GCF, it is unlikely that Park would have been invited to do this. In addition, Park has the opportunity to work to create an ecosystem around the GCF that makes Songdo a center of not only climate finance, but also related issues that the GCF should address, such as strengthening the institutional capacity of countries to receive funds. She can do this by promoting the GCF and Songdo to attract green financial entities and think tanks to locate there. This would be a task for future South Korean leaders, too, but Park could build momentum for this process.

Second, the external pressures that led Lee to pursue green growth in the first place are still present; in fact, some have increased. For example, under provisions agreed to during annual UN climate negotiations in Warsaw in 2013 and finalized in 2014, all 192 countries that are party to the UNFCCC are expected to submit national climate change plans, known as intended nationally determined contributions (INDCs), well before the December 2015 talks in Paris. Park announced at the 2014 UN Climate Summit that South Korea will submit an INDC.[34] Here, she can show leadership by crafting an ambitious but achievable INDC. That may be a difficult balance to strike, but the opportunity exists at a time when global climate talks have shifted to emphasize bottom-up contributions more than top-down targets and timetables.

THE PRICE OF A POST-2020 GLOBAL CLIMATE AGREEMENT: $10 BILLION AND COUNTING

At UN climate talks in Cancun in 2010, developed countries pledged to mobilize a collective total of $100 billion per year in new and additional funds by 2020 to assist developing countries with climate change mitigation and adaptation.[35] The decision to establish the GCF was finalized in 2011 at UN talks in Durban, South Africa. It was intended to be the primary vehicle for mobilizing this sum. The idea that developed countries would provide financial assistance to developing countries on climate change strategies dates back to the 1992 UNFCCC text, albeit with no specificity on timing or amounts. The centrality of money in global climate talks has only increased since then, with nearly every lower-income country asserting that its ability to address climate change depends on financial support.[36]

Climate finance and developing-country participation in climate change mitigation are inextricably linked and critical to the Paris negotiations, which will aim to achieve a successor regime to the Kyoto Protocol. Yvo de Boer, director general of the GGGI and former executive secretary of the UNFCCC, said in an interview that "comparability of effort" is the most important factor on which a successful outcome in Paris hinges.[37] "The major economies of the world—say, the G20—need to have the feeling that everyone is pulling their weight," he said.[38] The submission of INDCs may help on this point, but developing countries still demand funding to implement them. For example, Indian Environment Minister Prakash Javadekar has warned that without a "substantial" amount of climate finance from rich countries, developing countries may not submit their INDCs.[39] As de Boer said, "The large grouping of poor developing countries, who are probably insignificant in terms of their contribution to the problem, have to be given a sense that their effort means something and that they will be helped financially and technologically to make the transition [to a greener economy]."[40] A strong commitment to climate finance, specifically through government pledges to the GCF, is the price of an agreement in Paris in 2015.

By the conclusion of UN climate talks in Lima in December 2014, the GCF had won pledges totaling $10.2 billion, meeting the minimum level for initial capitalization of the fund that many experts agreed would demonstrate enough commitment to climate finance to provide a credible starting point for negotiations in Paris. This sum includes $100 million from South Korea (an increase from an initial pledge of $40 million). As of April 30, 2015, $4 billion of the $10.2 billion in pledges had been converted into signed contributions.[41]

There is much focus on the dollar amounts the GCF has been able to win so far, but this funding will be put to work at a time when the definition of climate finance is not settled. This lack of consensus made headlines in December 2014, when an Associated Press investigation revealed that Japan reported to the UN as "climate finance" a $1 billion loan to Indonesia to build three coal-fired power plants.[42] This triggered an outcry from NGOs, 250 of which requested in a letter to GCF Director Hela Cheikhrouhou that the fund explicitly exclude fossil fuels from acceptable climate finance activities.[43] Japan defended its investment in the plants, which will use newer, cleaner technology.[44]

Broadly speaking, climate finance refers to investments in mitigation, such as renewable energy technologies, or adaptation activities, which seek to reduce vulnerability to climate change effects. The latest figures released by the Climate Policy Initiative (CPI) showed $331 billion in global climate finance flows in 2013, $137 billion of which were public funds and $193 billion private investment, split almost evenly between developed and developing countries.[45] But a lack of parameters about what kinds of activities to include and the difficulty of tracking down data means that any estimates about climate finance are incomplete. The 2014 report by the UN's Intergovernmental Panel on Climate Change (IPCC) was the first to include a chapter on climate investment and finance; it noted "substantial" knowledge gaps in this area because "quantitative data are limited, relate to different concepts, and are incomplete."[46] The GCF will have to navigate this definitional ambiguity as it begins to deploy funds.

THE GREEN CLIMATE FUND

To assess whether South Korea's role as host of the Green Climate Fund can translate into greater influence on the global green growth agenda, it is important to consider the factors upon which the success of the fund itself will depend—in particular, private-sector funding, adaptation, and strengthening recipient countries' ability to access the fund, an issue known as "readiness." South Korea does not sit on the GCF board (it is an alternate member to China) and will have limited influence on its governance structure. However, there are avenues for the ROK to influence all three factors related to the GCF's future success through its role as host of the GGGI and the GCF.

One of the most important things to understand about the GCF is that it is expected to catalyze private-sector investment into mitigation and adaptation. It is widely recognized that the goal of mobilizing $100 billion per year in new and additional funds is not realistic without private-sector involvement. To attract this investment, the GCF board is designing a private-sector facility (PSF), a feature that will make it unique among climate funds. The PSF is intended to evolve into a financial entity; until then it will work through accredited intermediaries to disburse funds. To achieve this, the GCF has to deal head-on with a major barrier to climate finance: risk. The GCF board acknowledged this at its eighth board meeting in October 2014, stating, "Given the role of GCF funding to catalyze investments that are not otherwise occurring in mitigation and adaptation, GCF funding may naturally be exposed to higher risks, and possible losses."[47]

The crux of the challenge is to change the risk-reward profile in order to attract private funds. To that end, the GCF has formed a private-sector advisory group (PSAG) to provide advice on the design of the PSF. The PSAG's work revolves around three core questions.[48] First, what instruments should be used in interacting with the private sector?

On this question, the board adopted the PSAG's recommendation to include a broader array of financial instruments, beyond the grants and concessional loans allowed for in the GCF governing instrument.[49] The IPCC's latest climate change report concluded that, although there are case studies on the combinations of instruments that can attract private investment into mitigation and adaptation, "there is no general understanding of what are the efficient levers to mobilize private investment and its potential in any country (since they will differ by investment and country)."[50] The flexibility to choose from a broad array of financial instruments is important.

A second question for the PSAG is how to involve local private-sector actors in developing countries. Current research on climate finance illustrates why this is so important; the CPI report found that "investors favored domestic investment environments with which they were more familiar and which they perceived to be less risky. Private actors had an especially strong domestic investment focus with [$]174 billion or 90 [percent] of their investments remaining in the country of origin."[51] Finally, the PSAG is working on recommendations as to how to mobilize funds at scale. On this question, the PSAG has noted that "attracting investment on the basis of strong project pipelines that deliver on country priorities and [programs] is important. The private sector will only invest in bankable projects where the underlying assets can be assessed or otherwise hedged and where the risk/return profiles are attractive."[52] Investments in climate-related projects can face political or macroeconomic risks, as any investment might, as well as challenges related to institutional capacity and the overall business environment on the ground. Here, the GGGI may have a role to play to work with countries that hope to access GCF funds. As GGGI Director General de Boer said in an interview, "I really see an opportunity for us to work on developing bankable projects and working with countries to make the policy environment more conducive to investments."[53]

The GCF is required to aim for a balance between funding mitigation and adaptation activities, and to place an even greater focus on adaptation for the most vulnerable countries.[54] This means that the prevailing uncertainty surrounding the meaning of adaptation is highly relevant to judging the fund's success. Private investment in adaptation has been noted as one of the most important knowledge gaps in climate finance.[55] The CPI report found that only 7 percent of total climate finance flows went to adaptation projects, although this figure reflects only public sources of funds because reliable data on private investment in adaptation could not be secured.[56] The GCF has noted that it has "a particular opportunity to differentiate itself from other climate finance channels by catalyzing private-sector investments in adaptation, as these have to date focused primarily on mitigation."[57] Moreover, countries applying for adaptation funding from the GCF will have to show how their projects result in real adaptation effects.[58] The GCF itself has acknowledged the difficulty in measuring adaptation.[59]

When it comes to funding adaptation, South Korea's recent track record as a global convener on green growth may position it to influence this critical mainstay on the global climate agenda. Under Lee, the ROK hosted numerous conferences on green growth–related topics and placed green growth on the agenda when it hosted the G20 summit in 2010. Lee's administration also created the East Asia Climate Partnership to advance cooperation on climate-related issues. South Korea can build on this capacity in order to contribute to the GCF's challenging tasks on adaptation. Perceptions of the ROK as a leader in green growth, combined with the country's status as home to the GCF, provide an opening for Park to attract green financial and policy entities to Songdo for discussions about adaptation. If these organizations established a permanent presence there, Songdo could eventually become a center of study and innovation on these issues.

Many experts note that because local context is so essential for adaptation, local actors need to have a voice in how money is spent.[60] The fund's structure ensures that at least some of them will. Country ownership of climate-related projects is an important principle underlying the GCF's work. Each country that plans to access GCF funding should select a national designated authority (NDA) or "focal point" to serve as the main point of contact with the fund. As of April 17, 2015, 119 developing countries had identified an NDA or focal point.[61] Many of them are located within national ministries. NDAs and focal points should be able to ensure that projects are consistent with the country's overall climate plans and priorities and have the ability to work with multiple participants. Only projects that receive no objection from the NDA will be funded.[62] This arrangement bolsters local ownership and could ease funding decisions, but it also relies on one in-country entity that may or may not address domestic politics surrounding potential projects in a transparent manner.

Some experts have raised concerns about political risk and lack of institutional capacity that may inhibit the effective use of funds in some countries.[63] To address this challenge, the GCF is implementing a readiness program to help prepare countries to access the fund.[64] This program may provide an important pathway for South Korea to influence the global green growth agenda through the GGGI. In addition to strengthening the NDAs and focal points, the readiness program will help countries assess existing climate strategies, identify investment priorities, and support the development of project pipelines. These activities align with the GGGI's updated priorities for the next five years, which include moving toward implementation of the green growth plans it has helped develop and attracting green finance.[65] The GGGI's new Green Investment Advisory Services program aims to develop bankable projects in line with a country's green growth strategies and plans and "will also offer in-country support to create an effective enabling environment for green investment to take place."[66] Although the GGGI would be only one among many delivery partners to implement the GCF's readiness program, its current work may give it a natural starting point: of the twenty-seven countries that had requested readiness funds from the GCF as of December 9, 2014, five of them are also countries in which the GGGI is working.[67]

CONCLUSIONS

Green growth is a crowded playing field. The proliferation of organizations dedicated to its study and the primacy of finance in global climate talks attest to this fact. However, climate finance, and by extension the GCF, is also facing headwinds beyond its control. Global carbon dioxide emissions reached record levels in 2013.[68] Coal use is up in Germany and the United Kingdom.[69] There are serious moral arguments about whether carbon-intensive sources of energy are better than none at all for those who still lack access to any source of electricity.[70] South Korea will have to work hard to remain relevant on green growth. The country is nowhere close to the largest source of greenhouse gas emissions, nor does it command enough resources to achieve global green growth alone or even in concert with one or two other middle powers. The U.S. pledge of $3 billion to the Green Climate Fund, thirty times larger than the ROK's, was celebrated as "*the* game-changing moment" in the GCF's initial capitalization drive.[71] South Korea's power to influence the GCF, and green growth writ large, will not be a function of its financial resources. It will take more subtle forms that draw upon its middle-power identity, such as the committed work of the GGGI, the potential to be an exemplar by demonstrating success with its domestic green growth policies, and utilizing its convening power on green growth to advance the agenda.

Understanding adaptation better and mobilizing private-sector funding for such activities provide an important opening for South Korean influence. These tasks constitute uncharted territory in some ways; they require not just greater effort or political will, but the development of more knowledge. No country has a monopoly on policy options. This opens the way for a middle power such as South Korea to contribute. As host of the GCF, the country has a rare opportunity to build up Songdo as a center for knowledge development on the challenges related to the GCF's mission by attracting green financial and policy-oriented organizations. All of this will require strong national leadership willing to champion green growth. As the first South Korean president to inherit a comprehensive green growth law and new ROK-based green growth organizations, President Park's actions during the remainder of her term will have an important effect on the country's future role in global green growth.

South Korea as a Middle Power: Global Ambitions and Looming Challenges

Andrew O'Neil

In what respects do South Korea's middle-power aspirations intersect with its foreign policy? What are some of the important challenges the ROK confronts in sustaining its middle-power ambitions in the twenty-first century? These are important questions—not merely for those who are interested in South Korea's role in the world, but also for those who analyze middle powers as a class of actor in world politics. The study of middle powers has recently reemerged, including in Asia, where many have begun to appreciate that the U.S.-China relationship is only part of the story regarding significant power shifts in international relations. The degree of agency possessed by middle powers has become increasingly apparent in Asia, where China's rise, and Beijing's approach to territorial issues in particular, has triggered pushback from states in the region. This chapter, in short, seeks to answer: How sustainable is South Korea's middle-power vision?

South Korea's middle-power identity maps closely to its global foreign policy strategy, which has been in place since the early 1990s. In this sense, the link between what Kal Holsti has termed "national role conception" and the direction of South Korean foreign policy is strong.[1] This link reflects a similar pattern for other medium-size states that are established middle powers (such as Australia) and emerging middle powers (such as South Africa) that have sought to make a greater impact on international relations through proactive diplomacy, aimed principally at influencing multilateral outcomes. Yet the ROK's foreign policy ambitions have expanded coterminous with deteriorating security circumstances at the regional level. Although South Korea has pulled well ahead of North Korea across nearly every major indicator of national power and influence, Pyongyang's nuclear weapons inventory has introduced a new destabilizing element to the Korean peninsula. Moreover, China's growing great-power shadow and rising concern in

Seoul over what some see as Japan's determination to be more asser-
tive strategically have added to worries over Northeast Asia's security
landscape. The ROK-U.S. alliance is today more robust than ever, but
Washington and Seoul did experience some tense periods during the
first decade of the twenty-first century under the Roh Moo-hyun and
Bush administrations.

South Korea's global ambitions have flourished despite increasing challenges at the local level. This may appear slightly counterin-
tuitive; a country with finite resources and more demanding regional
circumstances could be assumed to be less ambitious globally. However, deepening participation and leadership on specific issues on
the global stage makes sense for South Korea, not only for reasons
of economic integration but also because Seoul knows that it needs
to attract significant international support to deal with the continuing challenges emanating from North Korea, including managing any
future transition to Korean reunification.

MIDDLE POWERS IN THEORY AND PRACTICE

The term *middle power* continues to be subject to debate in the literature. In particular, contention persists over whether the term has significant purchase as a descriptor in international affairs; critics maintain
that the criteria for defining which states are middle powers and which
are not remain elusive. Those critical of the moniker further argue that
it obscures the substantial differences among nongreat powers by pre-
supposing certain modes of behavior among them. Realists in particular remain doubtful of the middle-power category, which undermines
the basic case that all secondary powers in international relations are,
to a greater or lesser extent, subservient to the great powers. Even those
who do not subscribe to the realist paradigm are skeptical of the degree
of agency possessed by nongreat powers. This is especially apparent in
analysis of Asia's contemporary order by those who see the return to a
distinctly hierarchical system that has China at the apex.[2]

Yet the recent literature has reflected something of a renaissance
in middle-power theory. Much of this endorses the traditional definition of middle powers as those states—roughly twenty to twenty-five
of them—that possess the material capabilities to shape outcomes in
niche areas in the global governance sphere when acting in concert

with like-minded states. This extends the earlier pathbreaking work of scholars such as George Glazebrook and Carsten Holdbraad, who were writing during the Cold War period when middle powers were often seen as driving progress in international organizations and as a crucial bridge between the developed and developing worlds, as well as the two superpowers.[3] States such as Canada, Australia, and the Netherlands may have been U.S. allies, but they were regarded—by others as well as themselves—as possessing the necessary attributes to play an honest-broker role in promoting positive outcomes in niche diplomacy, typically in multilateral settings and including policy areas such as arms control and the environment.[4] This honest-broker role has its lineage in the ideas of sixteenth-century Italian philosopher Giovanni Botero, who maintained that middle powers (*mezano*) "are exposed neither to violence by their weakness nor to envy by their greatness, and their wealth and power being moderate, passions are less violent, ambition finds less support and license less provocation than in large states."[5]

Middle powers exhibit distinctive characteristics, most notably a preference for multipolarity, rules-based order, and institutions, as well as ideational traits underpinning their claim to be good international citizens. Historically, these traits have tended to be linked with democratic governance at home and the promotion of democratic principles abroad, although emerging middle powers such as South Africa and Turkey are not as focused as more traditional middle powers such as Australia and Canada on pushing liberal models of human rights abroad. Contributing to making the world a better place, including by addressing issues that do not relate directly to the national interest, is a salient hallmark of middle-power diplomacy. Australia's former Foreign Minister Gareth Evans— himself an ardent proponent of the middle-power concept—neatly captures this mindset: "I refuse to believe that Australia is just another also-ran country, focusing wholly on our own interests defined in the narrowest possible way, not really caring much about the wider world we live in, and deserving to be treated accordingly."[6] Although many of the core assumptions of middle-power theory map closely to liberal internationalism (namely, that interdependence promotes cooperation), constructivist theory has more recently made an important contribution. The pivotal role of middle powers as "norm entrepreneurs" in diffusing new ideas exerts a strong attraction for many analysts.[7]

One of the striking aspects of discussion about the merits or otherwise of the middle-power category is that while many in academia and think tanks remain dismissive of its descriptive utility, policymakers around the world remain attracted to the term. In one sense, this should not come as a surprise. For policymakers in countries that are clearly not great powers, but whose national role conception rejects the idea of them being "small" or even "secondary" states, embracing a middle-power identity possesses normative connotations that convey a profile in material-power terms below the great powers but a step up from the rest. An increasing number of states are explicitly using the term middle power to characterize their location in the international system and their foreign policy aspirations. In short, the moniker still enjoys a robust currency in international relations despite its definitional shortcomings.

In addition to unilateral declarations by a growing number of states that mirror their national-role conception as middle powers, one tangible example of the persistence of middle-power identity is the so-called MIKTA initiative. Formed in September 2013 at a meeting of the foreign ministers of Mexico, Indonesia, South Korea, Turkey, and Australia, the purpose of MIKTA was described by the ROK's foreign minister as "playing a bridging role between countries with different views on the international stage…and expanding their role in establishing a better world order by taking advantage of individual middle power countries' diplomatic assets and cooperative mechanisms."[8] The most recent meeting of MIKTA was held on the sidelines of the November 2014 G20 summit; the joint communiqué reaffirmed the group's intention to "play a bridging role between advanced countries and developing countries on key global issues."[9]

SOUTH KOREA AS A MIDDLE POWER: GLOBAL AND REGIONAL DIMENSIONS

Insecurity and a sense of vulnerability have traditionally been at the heart of South Korea's perspective of the outside world. Understandably for a country that is wedged between larger powers (the "shrimp among the whales") and has been invaded and conquered many times, the ROK is anxious about its long-term security. As Don Oberdorfer and Robert Carlin have observed, "geography has dealt Korea a particularly difficult role, with it suffering nine hundred invasions in its two thousand years of recorded history and five major periods of foreign occupation."[10] Since its formation in 1948, South Korea's foreign policy vision has grown to be global in scope. Although the Korean War was essentially a civil war, it was also an international conflict involving many nations. The provision of UN-sponsored forces to counter North Korea's invasion ensured that the Korean War had a strong global dimension. Although for Koreans it was a calamity, it was the first "limited" war of the Cold War era. Few of the participants had much of an appreciation of Korean history, but the United States and its allies appreciated the geopolitical significance of the peninsula and the major test that North Korea's invasion posed in containing communism internationally.[11]

For most of its existence, South Korea's primary preoccupation has been how best to deter North Korean aggression while coexisting peacefully with its capricious northern neighbor. This balancing act has been pursued by Seoul through a mixture of covert and high-profile diplomacy with Pyongyang and of crafting the ROK military into one of the most formidable fighting forces in the world. Strengthening the alliance with the United States has also been a major part of South Korea's national strategy. Over time, the U.S.-ROK security alliance has come to be characterized by increasing "ideological solidarity," which since the late 1980s has been reflected in a shared commitment to democratic principles and greater alignment of worldviews.[12]

The central challenge for successive ROK governments has been to persuade North Korean elites that coercion will be actively resisted while at the same time keeping the door open for meaningful inter-Korean dialogue, including on reunification. This has taken various forms—from Park Chung-hee's back-channel dialogue with Pyongyang to Kim Dae-jung's Sunshine Policy—each strategy yielding mixed results. North Korea's emergence as a nuclear weapon state has further complicated South Korean strategy by providing Pyongyang with enhanced coercive power during future crises and the potential ability to deter the United States—and, for that matter, China—from intervening militarily on the Korean peninsula. Some South Korean politicians have called for the reintroduction of U.S. tactical nuclear forces to ROK territory, and a smaller minority has even broached the possibility of reactivating South Korea's nuclear weapons program, which was abandoned in the late 1970s.[13] From Seoul's perspective, gaining U.S. and Chinese support to restrain Pyongyang from "using" its nuclear inventory as cover to conduct small-scale but highly destabilizing acts of violence (as in 2010) may become a more salient consideration over time.

Export-led economic growth has been the other major element of South Korea's postwar national strategy. Indeed, the size and global reach of the ROK economy is today the single most important capability underpinning South Korea's claim to middle-power status. It is easy to forget that the ROK's economy was smashed by the Korean War and that Seoul had to rebuild it from the ground up. After 1953, successive ROK administrations (particularly that of Park Chung-hee) built a system of "authoritarian developmentalism," in which the national security state partnered with major conglomerates (*chaebol*) to exercise strict control of the domestic labor market.[14] This model had unfortunate consequences for political and civil rights, but it produced stunning levels of economic growth, and the rate of absolute poverty dropped from just over 40 percent of all households in 1965 to just under 10 percent by 1980.[15] The fraught transition to democracy after Park Chung-hee's death in 1979 and recovery from the damaging regional economic crisis of 1997–98 tested South Korea, but Seoul's successful navigation of both challenges marked a significant milestone in the country's national development.

The alliance with the United States has been integral to South Korea's achieving goals of economic development and managing the threat from North Korea. The presence of U.S. conventional and (until 1991) nuclear forces on South Korean territory has provided Seoul with extended deterrence that has allowed successive governments to keep defense expenditures lower than they would otherwise have been able to. Apart from deterring North Korea, the U.S. presence in Northeast Asia has also provided Seoul with reassurance that a resurgent Japan and an increasingly confident China will be counterbalanced by Washington. In the current context, this is important because suspicion and hostility toward Tokyo run deep among many South Koreans, and although the ROK values its economic relationship with neighboring China, South Korean policymakers are undoubtedly aware of the need to maintain some distance strategically from Beijing.[16] As with many other U.S. allies, extended deterrence has furnished South Korea with an existential safety net that fosters confidence among policymakers that they can pursue a relatively independent foreign policy agenda. As was evident in the Roh Moo-hyun period, the confidence underlying this autonomy has at times even manifested itself in policies that run directly counter to Washington's policy preferences, including acute tensions with the George W. Bush administration in relation to North Korea policy.[17]

One South Korean analyst has argued that South Korea "is a late-comer to middle power activism."[18] A notable feature of the ROK's journey to middle-power status was the lag between the country's acquisition of capabilities that qualified it for entry into the "club" and the decision by South Korean elites to incorporate middle-power identity into national strategy. As early as 1966, the Park Chung-hee administration sought to play a role in developing regional governance architecture through sponsorship of the short-lived Asian Pacific Council, an early first step in the development of a distinctive regionalism in Asia.[19] The so-called Miracle on the Han River witnessed South Korea overtaking North Korea's GDP by the mid-1970s (at the latest), and by the mid-1980s the ROK economy had expanded to an annual GDP of more than $100 billion, surpassing a number of high-performing European economies, including Switzerland.[20]

Yet it was not until the early 1990s that South Korea's identity as a middle power began to crystallize fully. This was reflected in a growing number of statements by ROK elites that embraced a distinctively internationalist tone. These statements were increasingly aspirational in the sense that they envisaged Seoul playing a larger role outside the Northeast Asian region and thinking beyond the alliance with the United States as the primary reference point for national strategy. The sense that the ROK was a regional power with global interests became a substantive theme in foreign policy rhetoric under the Kim Young-sam administration. This was reflected by the emergence of a globalization (segyehwa) policy that sought to expand South Korea's global horizons in the wake of the country formally joining the United Nations in 1991 and becoming a leader in Asia's burgeoning regionalism, most notably the Asia-Pacific Economic Cooperation, which formed in 1989.[21] ROK elites believed that South Korea's growing economic heft required an increasingly global foreign policy. By 1994, when President Kim Young-sam articulated the segyehwa policy, South Korea's annual GDP ($508 billion, in constant 2005 U.S. dollars) had surpassed that of Australia ($462 billion), the Netherlands ($503 billion), and India ($417 billion).[22]

Therefore, measured in purely in material power terms, South Korea was clearly in the global ranks of middle powers. However, ideational themes were just as important in providing momentum for the development of the country's middle-power identity. The fact that South Korea has successfully navigated the dual transition from developing to developed economy and from authoritarian to democratic state appeared to provide elites with an important sense of legitimacy in their expressions of middle-power identity. This was evident under the successive administrations of Kim Dae-jung (1998–2003) and Roh Moo-hyun (2003–2008), both of which built on the segyehwa policy by more assertively pressing South Korea's middle-power profile. Then Foreign Minister Hong Soon-young noted in 1998 that "Korea in the twenty-first century must stand as an Asian power and a middle power…it must have a clear sense of what it can and cannot do as a middle power situated between the world's most powerful nations."[23]

This policy direction continued despite the significant pressures on the ROK economy flowing from the 1997–98 Asian Financial Crisis and the periodic nuclear crises on the Korean peninsula. Instead of creating tensions with its region-focused initiatives on the peninsula spawned by the Sunshine Policy and deeper involvement in Asia's multilateral architecture, Seoul's global activism seemed to complement its local leadership ambitions.[24] But there was more to the shift than an abstract desire to be a solid global citizen. In addition to developing a foreign policy more independent from the United States and cooperating with important actors beyond Northeast Asia, ROK elites were keen to develop South Korea's soft power. President Roh Moo-hyun's creation of a "national image committee" within the Office of the Prime Minister was followed by his successor Lee Myung-bak's instituting a "presidential committee on nation branding."[25]

Under Presidents Lee and Park Geun-hye, South Korea's middle-power identity has become more prominent and substantive in scope.[26] Significantly, this has led to ROK elites embracing some of the classical ideas of the middle-power worldview. Speaking at the G20 meeting in Seoul in 2010, South Korea's vice minister of foreign affairs and trade observed that

> The world now works not hierarchically, but in a networked fashion. In this world, no one can dictate what others have to do. In a networked world, a group of like-minded countries can lead a meaningful change in the world. They do so not by power, but

through creative ideas, a smart and flexible strategy, and moral leadership. Middle power countries are well positioned to lead this interconnected world. And South Korea stands ready and willing to do so.[27]

There is some evidence that middle-power identity has acquired traction outside the South Korean policymaking world; an East Asia Institute poll of South Koreans in 2010 showed that 76.8 percent of respondents viewed the ROK as a middle power and just over half agreed that South Korea "should play a bridging role between advanced countries and developing countries."[28] Over time, this growing middle-power identity has become more tightly integrated with the ROK's global ambitions.

ENVISAGING "GLOBAL KOREA": OPPORTUNITIES...AND CHALLENGES?

The raising of South Korea's global sights, beginning in the mid-1990s, entered an important stage in the late 2000s, which coincided with the advent of the Lee administration. Much of the conceptual and practical groundwork had been laid, but it was the articulation of the Global Korea initiative in 2009 that confirmed the ROK's arrival as a genuine contributor to the realm of middle-power diplomacy. The underlying philosophy of Global Korea drew on important aspects of previous administrations' segyehwa policy by—in the words of an official presidential document—envisaging "a Korea that leaves behind a habit of diplomacy narrowly geared to the Korean Peninsula, and adopts a more open and enterprising posture that sees the world as the appropriate platform for its foreign policy and national interest."[29] Lee's vision has been essentially reaffirmed by Park, and a particular emphasis has been placed on how eventual reunification with the North would strengthen Korea's global role.[30]

Rather than signifying a detachment from the U.S. alliance, Seoul's initiative dovetailed with the 2009 U.S.-ROK Joint Vision Statement, which "expanded alliance cooperation beyond the Korean Peninsula and enabled South Korea to contribute to new dimensions of international security."[31] This underscored and built on South Korean contributions to postconflict operations worldwide as well as initiatives in the area of cybersecurity, and widened cooperation with the increasingly global NATO alliance. The shift toward a globally oriented alliance with the United States was noteworthy in a historical context because traditionally it had been conceived and designed exclusively as an operationally focused alliance to deter and ultimately defeat North Korean military aggression. Although this purpose has not disappeared—and in many respects it has been reinforced since 2010 through initiatives such as the Extended Deterrence Policy Committee[32]—the conclusion in 2012 of the Korea-U.S. free trade agreement has added a more explicit economic dynamic to U.S.-ROK relations. It has, to quote President Park, "moved the United States closer to a comprehensive strategic alliance."[33]

The timing of the Global Korea initiative was significant for three interrelated reasons. First, it coincided with the announcement that the G20 would replace the G8 as the premier economic global governance institution. South Korea was a founding member of the G20, which was formed in 1999 as a result of Canadian leadership and had its inaugural leaders' summit in Washington in 2008. In 2010, South Korea became the first non-G8 country to host the annual G20 leaders' summit in Seoul. A hallmark of the ROK's preparation for the summit was the role of developing states in crafting the agenda and moving it toward discussing alternative models of development to those of the West; the South Korean model (predictably) loomed large.[34] The emergence of the so-called Seoul Development Consensus focused less on the delivery of aid from the developed world to developing countries and more on "structurally important pillars of development like education and skills, infrastructure, domestic mobilization of resources, private sector–led growth, social inclusion, and food security."[35] South Korea has maintained a strong emphasis on development at subsequent G20 meetings, including at the 2014 leaders' summit in Brisbane.

Second, the Global Korea strategy was unveiled at the same time that Seoul articulated the New Asian Initiative that staked a claim for greater South Korean leadership in the region.[36] A major theme in the Lee government's rhetoric was an aspiration for the ROK to act on behalf of other Asian states in international forums. As President Lee stated, "Korea is capable enough to become a leader in Asia and represent the continent on the global stage."[37] In practical terms, this translated into a more integrated approach by Seoul to developing closer economic, security, and political ties with Southeast Asian states and expanding South Korea's footprint in the Association of Southeast Asian Nations

(ASEAN), both as an existing formal dialogue partner and also in terms of more intimate bilateral relations with strategic ASEAN countries Vietnam, Singapore, and Myanmar.[38] The nomenclature of the New Asian Initiative passed with the end of the Lee administration in 2013, but its thrust has been continued under President Park and expanded with her government's highly ambitious Eurasia Initiative, which envisages "making Eurasia into a single united continent, a continent of creativity and a continent of peace."[39]

Third, Global Korea emerged as the ROK made the significant transition in 2009 from being a net recipient of aid to being a net donor of official development assistance, the first state to have achieved this transition. The same year, South Korea joined the OECD's twenty-seven-member Development Assistance Committee, whose mission is to both coordinate ODA and promote global economic and social development.[40] Significantly, the ROK's ODA budget has increased above the DAC member average, despite tough economic conditions at home and ongoing aid program deliveries to North Korea, which Seoul does not count as part of its ODA budget.[41] This transition from being a recipient of ODA to a major donor has been significant because it provides credibility to Seoul's claim to be a bridge between the developed and developing worlds, a central feature of South Korea's middle-power identity and global strategy.

South Korea's progress toward achieving its vision of being a global middle power has been impressive, but how sustainable is this vision over the long term? In particular, what are some of the challenges that the ROK will confront in sustaining its middle-power ambitions in the twenty-first century? Although there is a significant amount of research on how great powers rise and fall throughout history, there has been little on the rise and fall of middle powers. One observer has argued that Canada has declined as a middle power because of its unwillingness to challenge U.S. policy on global issues.[42] Another analyst has claimed Australia is in danger of slipping down the world rankings of material power, including military expenditure.[43] However, there is little systematic analysis of the pitfalls faced by middle powers in sustaining their ambitions over time.

One prominent challenge relates to the risk of "middle power overstretch," which borrows its logic from Paul Kennedy's notion of "imperial overstretch," where great powers decline (in part) due to an overextension of commitments that they cannot deliver. It stands to reason that middle powers in international relations are susceptible to the same fate. This has been discussed in the Australian context; one analyst observed that under the Rudd government (2007–2013), Australia risked "pursuing solutions to problems which it lacks the capacity to resolve."[44] The danger for middle powers is that stated diplomatic ambitions will be beyond the capacity of policymakers either because they lack the resources to achieve tangible outcomes or because the country's diplomatic focus is not strategically focused on a given issue area. The Rudd government's failure to deliver on its promise to lead the development of an Asia-Pacific Security Cooperation forum was due in no small part to its inability to persuade other regional states to support the initiative in a period when Australia's diplomatic agenda was widening without a commensurate investment in the country's foreign service.[45]

Seoul remains ambitious in proposing initiatives as part of its activist middle-power agenda, but it is unclear whether it has the ability to maintain a focus on completing this agenda over time. Should certain initiatives that have been promised as part of foreign policy not be pursued further as part of an integrated strategy—President Park's recent Eurasia Initiative comes to mind—South Korea may confront something of a credibility deficit in its foreign policy, which in turn will make it harder to propose future initiatives as part of a broader middle-power strategy. As one recent study has noted, Seoul does not have a good track record of building sustainable multilateral architecture in Northeast Asia, despite repeated attempts by successive governments since the early 1990s.[46] Moreover, MIKTA notwithstanding, South Korea's capacity to sustain its leadership over time at the global multilateral level will be tested, even assuming that policymakers maintain their normative commitment to middle-power identity.

Sustaining commitment over time is one challenge, but another task for South Korea will be to sustain its middle-power contribution to multilateral diplomacy at the global level. The most salient and persistent obstacle to this is North Korea. Pyongyang continues to pose an existential threat to South Korea's security, the magnitude of which has been accentuated by the North's acquisition of nuclear weapons. North Korea may not intend to launch major strikes or a full-scale invasion against the South, but as the *Cheonan* and Yeonpyeong attacks in 2010 illustrated, the regime in Pyongyang remains extremely capable of carrying out military provocations that fall under the threshold of all-out conflict. Indeed, one of the most pressing challenges for Seoul and Washington has been to develop plans to quickly and decisively respond to these provocations without escalating to full-scale war. However, as North Korea's nuclear inventory grows, and as the country's leadership becomes more confident about being able to deliver these weapons against a host of targets in Northeast Asia, Pyongyang will almost certainly feel increasingly emboldened to use coercion to achieve foreign policy objectives. As a regime that thrives on international tension to justify its claims of legitimacy at home, North Korea's leadership has few incentives to promote stability in the region, so it is highly probable that its crisis-driven approach to the Korean peninsula will continue.

For Seoul, a refractory northern neighbor undermines its capacity to pursue a global middle-power role in two important respects. The first is that ROK public opinion will be less likely to directly support international initiatives that yield few direct payoffs for South Korea in a context whereby its security and prosperity are being directly compromised. As Sook-Jong Lee points out, "public support for peacekeeping activities tends to decrease quickly when tension between the two Koreas rises."[47] Among the general public, countering immediate threats from North Korea will invariably trump more abstract notions of pursuing good international citizenship. The second factor (as noted earlier) is that Seoul will struggle to achieve its global agenda if policymakers are preoccupied with addressing the North Korean threat for extended periods of time. So far, South Korea has managed this parallel challenge adeptly (the 2010 G20 summit occurred the same month as the Yeonpyeong attacks), but a serious protracted crisis on the peninsula would make life extremely difficult for those charged with pursuing the Global Korea strategy. Tensions and crises with Pyongyang also raise inevitable questions about the credibility of statements by ROK officials linking reunification with a more global Korea. The bottom line is that Pyongyang has no stake in supporting South Korea's global ambitions—in fact, to the contrary—and North Korean behavior will continue to constrain the extent to which Seoul is able to drive progress towards Korean reunification, irrespective of how much support it enjoys internationally.

The second looming challenge the ROK will face in sustaining its middle-power ambitions is negotiating the influence of the great powers, in particular China and the United States. South Korea has succeeded in carving out more autonomy from Washington and Beijing in foreign policy terms—thus mitigating Korea's historical situation of being squeezed by materially stronger powers—but the reality is that this autonomy has limits. In particular, balancing middle-power aspirations with alliance obligations can be seen as challenging, and many emerging middle powers have taken positions on some issues at odds with Washington. How enthusiastic will future governments in Seoul be in pursuing policies at the global level that run counter to the preferences of its long-standing security alliance partner? Deteriorating relations between Washington and Beijing would be especially damaging to South Korea's global middle-power aspirations. Having to choose sides between Asia's great powers is an unsavory scenario for all regional states that have an alliance with Washington and large-scale trade and investment ties with Beijing, but it is an especially undesirable prospect for South Korea. ROK elites understand well that China's influence on the Korean peninsula will endure and that Beijing will play a crucial role in shaping North Korea's future, including in any future reunification settlement. At the same time, the U.S. alliance continues to be central to South Korea's national strategy in myriad ways, not least because it hedges against China's rising influence.[48]

CONCLUSIONS

Like many other middle powers, South Korea is searching for equilibrium in its international environment. As Hedley Bull argued in the early 1970s, medium-size states will always seek to promote cooperation among the great powers while striving to avoid being dominated by a concert of powers.[49] As South Korea's material power has grown, so too have the foreign policy ambitions of its elites. Today, the ROK's national role conception as a middle power is inseparable from the global agenda that drives much of the country's foreign policy. As is the case with many other middle powers, the U.S. alliance provides Seoul with the necessary strategic cover to pursue an increasingly ambitious global agenda. But there remain other challenges and potential pitfalls for South Korea. These include exposing a credibility deficit in foreign policy by failing to sustain the country's active middle-power role over time and falling short of being able to manage the potentially competing demands of global ambitions and demonstrating continued loyalty to South Korea's security ally, the United States.

Most notably, however, the unpredictable threat from a nuclear-armed North Korea provides a constant reality check for ROK policy elites that, in a policy sense, regional challenges will always be more pressing and immediate than those at the global level. This is not to say that successive South Korean governments have overlooked this privately, but it is fair to say that South Korea's diplomatic successes have been more high profile in global multilateral forums than in Northeast Asia. Of course, managing the North Korean issue and pursuing a global agenda are not mutually exclusive given the international implications of Pyongyang's nuclear program. The point to emphasize is that unlike other peer states in the international system, South Korea is unlikely to ever enjoy the luxury of a tranquil regional environment as it seeks to further cement its place as a global middle power in the twenty-first century.

Endnotes

SOUTH KOREA AS A MIDDLE POWER IN GLOBAL GOVERNANCE: "PUNCHING ABOVE ITS WEIGHT" BASED ON NATIONAL ASSETS AND DYNAMIC TRAJECTORY

1. Martin Albrow, "Summits as Narratives Between Leaders and Their Publics," in *Toward the Consolidation of the G20: From Crisis Committee to Global Steering Committee*, ed. Colin I. Bradford and Wonhyuk Lim (Seoul: Korea Development Institute and Brookings Institution, 2010), pp. 394–402.
2. Stewart Patrick, "The G20: Shifting Coalitions of Consensus Rather than Blocs," in *Toward the Consolidation of the G20*, pp. 358–370.
3. Norman D. Levin and Yong-Sup Han, *The Shape of South Korea's Future: South Korean Attitudes Toward Unification and Long Term Security Issues* (Santa Monica: RAND Corporation, 1999).
4. Colin I. Bradford Jr., *From Trade-Driven Growth to Growth-Driven Trade: Reappraising the East Asian Development Experience* (Paris: OECD, 1994).
5. Changyong Rhee and Alok Sheel, "The Role of Emerging Economies in Major G-20 Initiatives," in *The G-20 Summit at Five: Time for Strategic Leadership*, ed. Kemal Dervis and Peter Drysdale (Washington, DC: Brookings Institution Press, 2014).
6. Global Green Growth Institute (GGGI), *Green Growth in Motion: Sharing South Korea's Experience* (Seoul: GGGI, 2011), based on *The Right Way to Know about Green Growth*, ed. Kim Hyung Kook (Seoul: Nanam and Presidential Committee on Green Growth, 2011).
7. Cheonsik Woo, ed., *Global Green Growth Summit 2011: Building Planet-Responsible Civilization*, proceedings, June 20–21, 2011 (Seoul: Korea Development Institute, 2011).
8. Colin I. Bradford, "Shifting the Political Dynamics in 2015–2016: Strengthening Global Leadership and Governance by Moving an Integrated Global Agenda Forward: Implications for Turkey and China," draft manuscript now in circulation (Washington, DC: Brookings Institution, January 2015).
9. Article 1, Korea Foundation Act, https://en.kf.or.kr/?menuno=524.

DEVELOPMENT EFFECTIVENESS: CHARTING SOUTH KOREA'S ROLE AND CONTRIBUTIONS

1. Official development assistance (ODA) Korea, *History of Korea's ODA* (2013), http://www.odakorea.go.kr/index.jsp. Unless otherwise noted, all currency is in U.S. dollars.

2. Eun Mee Kim, *Big Business, Strong State: Collusion and Conflict in South Korean Development, 1960-1990* (New York: State University of New York Press, 1997).

3. Hong-min Chun, Elijah N. Munyi, and Heejin Lee, "South Korea as an Emerging Donor: Challenges and Changes on Its Entering OECD/DAC," *Journal of International Development* 22, no. 6, 2010, p. 798.

4. Eun Mee Kim, Pil Ho Kim, and Jinkyung Kim, "From Development to Development Cooperation: Foreign Aid, Country Ownership, and the Developmental State in South Korea," *Pacific Review* 26, no. 3, 2013, p. 314.

5. Chun et al., "South Korea as an Emerging Donor," p. 790.

6. Knowledge Sharing Program (KSP), *Bilateral Consultation*, 2013, http://www.ksp.go.kr/.

7. Ibid.

8. Moctar Aboubacar, "Emerging Donors and Knowledge Sharing for Development: The Case of Korea," *Yonsei Journal of International Studies* 9, no. 1, 2014, p. 227.

9. Knowledge Sharing Program.

10. Yulan Kim and MoonJoong Tcha, "Introduction to the Knowledge Sharing Program (KSP) of Korea," *Korea Compass* (Washington, DC: Korea Economic Institute of America, 2012), pp. 3–4, http://keia.org/publication/introduction-knowledge-sharing-program-ksp-korea.

11. EDCF, *EDCF Annual Report 2013* (Seoul: EDCF, 2013).

12. Ibid., p. 28.

13. Seungjoo Lee, "Multilayered World Order and South Korea's Middle Power Diplomacy: The Case of Development Cooperation Policy," EAI MPDI Working Paper (Seoul: East Asian Institute, 2014), p.18.

14. Ibid.

15. Korean Overseas International Cooperation Agency (KOICA), 2013.

16. Kang-ho Park, "Korea's Role in Global Development," Brookings East Asia Commentary no. 36, February 2010, http://www.brookings.edu/research/opinions/2010/02/09-korea-global-development.

17. World Friends Korea website, http://www.worldfriendskorea.or.kr/.

18. Terrence Roehrig, "South Korea, Foreign Aid, and UN Peacekeeping: Contributing to International Peace and Security as a Middle Power," *Korea Observer* 44, no. 4, 2013, p. 632.

19. World Friends Korea website.

20. Ibid.

21. Roehrig, "South Korea, Foreign Aid, and UN Peacekeeping," p. 632.

22. Chun et al., "South Korea as an Emerging Donor," p. 790.

23. Seamus Taggart, "South Korea: Rejuvenating the Traditional Aid," *Italian Institute for International Political Studies,* September 3, 2014, http://www.ispionline.it/en/pubblicazione/south-korea-rejuvenating-traditional-aid-10211.

24. S. Lee, "Multilayered World Order and South Korea's Middle Power Diplomacy," pp. 16–23.

25. Ibid., p. 16.

26. Organization for Economic Cooperation and Development (OECD) Development Assistance Committee (DAC) Peer Review of Korea (Paris: OECD, 2012), http://www.oecd.org/dac/peerreviewsofdacmembers/Korea%20CRC%20-%20FINAL%2021%20JAN.pdf.

27. Ministry of Foreign Affairs (MOFA) ODA/Development Cooperation, http://www.mofa.go.kr/ENG/policy/oda/index.jsp?menu=m_20_110.

28. Roehrig, "South Korea, Foreign Aid, and UN Peacekeeping."

29. S. Lee, "Multilayered World Order and South Korea's Middle Power Diplomacy," p. 17.

30. Lean Alfred Santos, "South Korea Increases ODA, Pushes for 'Win-Win' Foreign Aid Policy," *Devex*, January 14, 2014, https://www.devex.com/news/south-korea-increases-oda-pushes-for-win-win-foreign-aid-policy-82653.
31. "Seoul's ODA Budget Jumps 9 Percent for Next Year," Yonhap News, September 18, 2014, http://english.yonhapnews.co.kr/national/2014/09/18/83/0301000000AEN201 40918009100315F.html.
32. "S. Korea's Development Aid to Rise 5 Percent This Year," Yonhap News, January 9, 2015, http://english.yonhapnews.co.kr/national/2015/01/09/80/0301000000AEN2015010 9006000315F.html.
33. OECD DAC 2012, p. 11.
34. MOFA ODA.
35. OECD DAC 2012, p. 11.
36. Ibid.
37. K. Park, "Korea's Role in Global Development."
38. MOFA ODA.
39. Ibid.
40. Philipp Olbrich and David Shim, "South Korea as a Global Actor: International Contributions to Development and Security," GIGA Focus no. 2 (Hamburg: German Institute of Global and Area Studies), p. 2, http://www.giga-hamburg.de/en/system/files/publications/gf_international_1202.pdf.
41. Eun Mee Kim and Jae Eun Lee, "Busan and Beyond: South Korea and the Transition from Aid Effectiveness to Development Effectiveness," *Journal of International Development* 25, no. 6, 2013, pp. 787–89.
42. Ibid., p. 788.
43. OECD DAC 2012, p. 11.
44. Seong Hoon Lee, Moon Suk Hong, and Hanee Kang, "The Outcomes and Future Challenges of the Busan HLF-4: CSOs' Perspectives," Busan Global Civil Society Forum, Issue Brief 2, February 2012, p. 5, http://kofid.org/en/bbs_view.php?no=1262&code=news.
45. Sung-Hoon Park, "South Korea and the European Union: A Promising Partnership for Development Cooperation?" ESP European Strategic Partnerships Observatory Policy Brief, November 15, 2014, p. 3.
46. Kim and Lee, "Busan and Beyond," pp. 792–93.
47. Olbrich and Shim, "South Korea as a Global Actor," p. 3.
48. OECD DAC 2012.
49. Thomas Kalinowski and Hyekyung Cho, "Korea's Search for a Global Role Between Hard Economic Interests and Soft Power," *European Journal of Development Research* 24, 2012, p. 250.
50. S. Lee, "South Korea's Middle Power Diplomacy," p. 20.
51. Lee, Hong, and Kang, "The Outcomes and Future Challenges of the Busan HLF-4," 2012, p. 6.
52. Kim and Lee, "Busan and Beyond," p. 799.
53. MOFAT 2009.
54. Vincent Darracq and Daragh Neville, "South Korea's Engagement in Sub-Saharan Africa Fortune, Fuel and Frontier Markets" (Chatham House, October 2014), p. 2.
55. OECD DAC 2012.
56. S. Park, "South Korea and the European Union," p. 1.
57. Santos, "South Korea Increases ODA."
58. Sojung Yoon, "*Saemaul Undong* Becomes Global Development Model," Korea.net, October 23, 2014, http://www.korea.net/NewsFocus/Policies/view?articleId=122360.

59. Sooyoung Park, "Analysis of *Saemaul Undong*: A Korean Rural Development Programme in the 1970s," *Asia-Pacific Development Journal* 16, no. 2, 2009, p. 116.

60. K. K. Lee, *Hangugedaehan kaebalwŏnjowa hyŏmnyŏk* [Development Assistance and Cooperation to South Korea: A Review of ODA for South Korea as a Recipient and Case Studies] (Seoul: KOICA, 2004), pp. 29–34.

61. Jae-Jung Suh and Jinkyung Kim, "Aid to Build Governance in a Fragile State: Foreign Assistance to a Post-Conflict Korea," in *Post-Conflict Development in East Asia*, ed. Brendan M. Howe (Farnham: Ashgate, 2014), pp. 67–68.

62. Ma Young Sam, Jung-he Song, and Dewey E. Moore, "Korea's Public Diplomacy: A New Initiative for the Future," Asan Policy Institute Issue Brief no. 39, 2012, http://en.asaninst.org/contents/issue-brief-no-39-koreas-public-diplomacy-a-new-initiative-for-the-future.

63. Nicholas J. Cull, "'Building Ideas': Making Korean Public Diplomacy Work," *Public Diplomacy Magazine,* summer 2013, p. 17, http://publicdiplomacymagazine.com/issue-brief-bulging-ideas-making-korean-public-diplomacy-work.

64. Kim et al., "From Development to Development Cooperation," p. 315.

65. Chun et al., "South Korea as an Emerging Donor," p. 799.

66. OECD DAC 2012.

67. Jin-Wook Choi, "From a Recipient to a Donor State: Achievements and Challenges of Korea's ODA," *International Review of Public Administration* 15, no. 3, 2010, p. 42; Anselmo Lee, *Post-Busan and New Paradigm for International Development Cooperation,* 2012, p. 977, https://www.kdevelopedia.org/resource/view/04201408040133449.do#; S. Lee, "South Korea's Middle Power Diplomacy," p. 41; S. Park, "South Korea and the European Union," p. 2.

68. Aboubacar, "Emerging Donors and Knowledge Sharing for Development," p. 225.

69. Chun et al., "South Korea as an Emerging Donor," p. 794.

70. Kalinowski and Cho, "Korea's Search," pp. 243, 249.

71. Government of Korea (GOK), *Strategic Plan for International Development Co-operation* (Seoul: GOK, 2010); Prime Minister's Office, *The Mid-Term ODA Policy for 2011-2015* (Seoul: PMO, 2010).

72. Prime Minister's Office, *The Mid-Term ODA Policy for 2011-2015.*

73. OECD Query Wizard, International Development Statistics, 2013, http://stats.oecd.org/qwids.

74. Santos, "South Korea Increases ODA."

75. Aboubacar, "Emerging Donors and Knowledge Sharing for Development," p. 228.

76. K. Park, "Korea's Role in Global Development."

77. Olbrich and Shim, "South Korea as a Global Actor," p. 4.

78. Chun et al., "South Korea as an Emerging Donor," p. 792; A. Lee, "Post-Busan and New Paradigm for International Development Cooperation," p. 986.

79. Darracq and Neville, "South Korea's Engagement in Sub-Saharan Africa," pp. 2–3.

80. Soyeun Kim, "Bridging Troubled Worlds? An Analysis of the Ethical Case for South Korean Aid," *Journal of International Development* 23, no. 6, 2011, p. 811.

81. S. Lee, "South Korea's Middle Power Diplomacy," p. 3.

82. M. A. Rudderham, "Middle Power Pull: Can Middle Powers use Public Diplomacy to Ameliorate the Image of the West?," YCISS Working Paper no. 46 (Toronto: York Centre for International and Security Studies, 2008), p. 2.

83. Kalinowski and Cho, "Korea's Search," p. 249.

84. K. Park, "Korea's Role in Global Development."

85. OECD DAC 2012, p. 20.

86. Ibid.

87. Chun et al., "South Korea as an Emerging Donor," p. 792.
88. Kim, "Bridging Troubled Waters?," p. 809; OECD DAC 2012, pp. 15–17.
89. Kalinowski and Cho, "Korea's Search for a Global Role," p. 249.
90. Chun et al., "South Korea as an Emerging Donor," p. 799; Kim, "Bridging Troubled Worlds?," p. 808; Lee, "Post-Busan and New Paradigm for International Development Cooperation," p. 985.
91. Santos, "South Korea Increases ODA."
92. EDCF, *Annual Report 2003* (Seoul: EDCF, 2003).
93. Ibid., p. 9.
94. EDCF, *Annual Report 2004* (Seoul: EDCF, 2004), p. 11.
95. Ibid.; EDCF, *Annual Report 2005* (Seoul: EDCF, 2005), p. 11.
96. Figure 3, EDCF 2013, p. 26
97. EDCF 2013; International Development Cooperation Committee 2014.
98. EDCF 2003, p. 32.
99. EDCF 2013, p. 78.
100. Eximbank 2014.
101. EDCF 2004, p.14.
102. Taggart, "South Korea."
103. Lee, Hong, and Kang, "The Outcomes and Future Challenges of the Busan HLF-4," 2012, p. 5.
104. Kim and Lee, "Busan and Beyond," p. 796.
105. K. Park, "Korea's Role in Global Development."
106. OECD DAC 2012, p. 14.
107. Ibid., p. 17.
108. Taggart, "South Korea."
109. OECD DAC 2012, p. 13.
110. Aboubacar, "Emerging Donors and Knowledge Sharing for Development," p. 299.
111. S. Lee, "South Korea's Middle Power Diplomacy," p. 11.
112. Ibid., pp. 2–3.

NUCLEAR GOVERNANCE: SOUTH KOREA'S EFFORTS TO STRENGTHEN REGIMES AND FRAMEWORKS FOR THE SAFE AND SECURE USE OF NUCLEAR ENERGY

1. See Nuclear Suppliers Group Plenary Meeting Press Statement, May 22–23, 2003, Busan, South Korea, http://www.nuclearsuppliersgroup.org/images/Files/Documents-page/Public_Statements/2003-07-press-busan.pdf.
2. Agreement for Cooperation, National Nuclear Security Administration, http://nnsa.energy.gov/sites/default/files/nnsa/05-13-multiplefiles/2013-05-02%20Korea_South_123.pdf.
3. Korea Electric Power Company Monthly Report, January 2015.
4. David Adam Stott, "South Korea's Global Nuclear Ambitions," *Asia-Pacific Journal*, March 22, 2010.
5. Mark Holt, "U.S. and South Korean Cooperation in the World Nuclear Energy Market: Major Policy Considerations," Congressional Research Service Report, June 25, 2013.
6. World Nuclear Association, "Nuclear Power in South Korea," http://www.world-nuclear.org/info/Country-Profiles/Countries-O-S/South-Korea.
7. Of course, the 2011 Fukushima accident led to a major global slowdown in nuclear energy growth, as concerned publics demanded more safety assurances and

oversight of nuclear industry. This was the case in Korea, too, and in 2014 the government issued a revised nuclear energy plan that scaled back significantly the number of new nuclear reactors.

8. Cheon Seong-whun, "Setting the Agenda for the Success of the Nuclear Security Summit in Seoul," *Korea Focus*, 2011; Jun Bong-Geun, "Road to the 2012 Seoul Nuclear Security Summit," U.S.-Korea Institute Working Paper, 2012, p. 8.

9. Ser Myo-ja, "Lee Invites a Nuke-Free North Korea to 2012 Security Summit," *Joong-gAng Ilbo*, April 15, 2010.

10. Kim Mi-Kyung, "Next Year's Seoul Nuclear Security Summit…North Korea Nuclear Issue Excluded?" [*Ne nyeon Seoul haek-anbojungsanghui-ui…Bukhan-eun eobta.*"], *Seoul Shinmun*, February 1, 2011.

11. Jun, "Road to the 2012 Seoul Nuclear Security Summit."

12. G. John Ikenberry and Mo Jongryn, *The Rise of Korean Leadership* (New York: Palgrave Macmillan, 2013); Duyeon Kim, "2012 Nuclear Security Summit: The Korean Twist," Korea Economic Institute Academic Paper Series, September 2011; Hahn Choong-hee, "Seoul Nuclear Security Summit—A Quantum Leap in Korea's Diplomacy," Ministry of Foreign Affairs, March 21, 2012; and Jun, "Road to the 2012 Seoul Nuclear Security Summit."

13. White House Office of the Press Secretary, Communique of the Washington Nuclear Security Summit, 2010, https://www.whitehouse.gov/the-press-office/communiqu-washington-nuclear-security-summit; and 2012 Seoul Nuclear Security Summit, Seoul Communique, http://www.nss2014.com/sites/default/files/documents/seoul_communique_final.pdf.

14. Miles Pomper, "The Seoul Nuclear Security Summit: How Much of a Success?," Korea Economic Institute Academic Paper Series, May 23, 2012, pp. 3–4.

15. Pomper, "The Seoul Nuclear Security Summit," p. 3.

16. Ikenberry and Mo, *The Rise of Korean Leadership*, pp. 134, 132.

17. Jun, "Road to the 2012 Seoul Nuclear Security Summit," pp. 14–18.

18. Author interview with U.S. official, February 4, 2015.

19. Ikenberry and Mo, *The Rise of Korean Leadership*, pp. 118, 130.

20. Asan Institute for Policy Studies, "MOU Between the Asan Institute for Policy Studies and the Korean Nuclear Society," http://en.asaninst.org/contents/mou-between-the-asan-institute-for-policy-studies-and-the-korean-nuclear-society.

21. Choe Sang-Hun, "Scandal in South Korea Over Nuclear Revelations," *New York Times*, August 3, 2013.

22. Shin Chang-hoon, "The 2014 Hague Nuclear Security Summit and Korea's Duty" [*2014-nyeon Hei-geu haek-anbojeongsanghui-ui-wa uri-ui chaekmu*], Asan Institute for Policy Studies Issue Brief, 2013.

SOUTH KOREA'S ROLE AS HOST OF THE GREEN CLIMATE FUND: IMPLICATIONS FOR ROK CONTRIBUTIONS TO GREEN GROWTH

1. "Keeping the Show on the Road," *Economist*, December 14, 2014.

2. For a good overview of this topic, see Suh Yong-Chung, "Post-2020 Climate Change Regime Formation: An Advanced Developing Country's Perspective," in *Post-2020 Climate Change Regime Formation*, ed. Suh-Yong Chung (New York: Routledge, 2013).

3. The Bali Action Plan included a proposal for developing countries to submit "nationally appropriate mitigation actions" (NAMAs), which can differ by country according to the unique circumstances of each.

4. Katia Karousakis, Burno Gay, and Cedric Philibert, *Differentiating Countries in Terms of Mitigation Commitments and Actions and Support* (OECD/IEA, 2008), http://www.oecd.org/env/cc/41762372.pdf.

5. Jeremy Tamanini, *The Global Green Economy Index*, 4th ed., October 2014, p. 43. The GGEI measures thirty-two indicators and datasets within four dimensions: leadership and climate change, efficiency sectors, markets and investment, and environmental and natural capital.

6. For example, see Green Growth Best Practice initiative (GGBP), *Green Growth in Practice: Lessons from Country Experiences*, 2014, p. 45, which notes that in South Korea and other countries where green growth policies have been implemented, "economic growth trajectories have not been fundamentally altered."

7. "Breach of Promise," *Korea Times*, September 3, 2014.

8. The U.S. Department of Energy's Carbon Dioxide Information Analysis Center measures CO_2 emissions from fossil fuels and cement manufacture; by this measure, the center estimated that South Korea's emissions were 164 million metric tons in 2011 and 166 million metric tons in 2012 (preliminary estimate).

9. Ernst and Young Renewable Energy Country Attractiveness Index (RECAI), September 2014, a quarterly measure of forty countries, http://www.ey.com/UK/en/Industries/Cleantech/Renewable-Energy-Country-Attractiveness-Index.

10. "KEPCO set to export smart grid technologies," *Korea Times*, October 27, 2014.

11. Woo Jin Chung, "Update on ROK Energy Sector and Energy Policies," NAPNet Special Reports, July 21, 2014.

12. Global Green Growth Institute (GGGI), *GGGI Strategic Plan 2015-2020: Accelerating the Transition to a New Model of Growth*, November 2014; "Addressing the Social Implications of Green Growth," OECD/Green Growth Knowledge Platform Sustainable Development Forum, Paris, November 13–14, 2014.

13. Tamanini, Global Green Economy Index, p. 9.

14. For example, see OECD, *Green Growth Indicators 2014*, OECD Green Growth Studies (Paris: OECD Publishing, 2014); or GGBP, *Green Growth in Practice*.

15. For example, see Lee Myung-bak's discussion of green growth as a "me first" strategy in his article "Shifting Paradigms: The Road To Global Green Growth," *Global Asia* 4, no. 4, winter 2010, pp. 8–12.

16. The United States never ratified the Kyoto Protocol, and China, classified as a developing country, has no obligations to cut greenhouse gas emissions under the protocol.

17. White House Office of the Press Secretary, "FACT SHEET: U.S.-China Joint Announcement on Climate Change and Clean Energy Cooperation," November 11, 2014.

18. PBL Netherlands Environmental Assessment Agency/European Commission Joint Research Center, "Trends in Global Co2 Emissions: 2013 Report," p. 14.

19. For more discussion on middle powers' pursuit of influence in niche areas, see Sook-Jong Lee, "South Korea as New Middle Power Seeking Complex Diplomacy," EAI Asia Security Initiative Working Paper, September 2012.

20. "S. Korea to Raise Eco-Friendly Support to 30 Percent of ODA by 2020," Yonhap News, June 21, 2012.

21. List of KOICA's Green Growth Projects, provided by KOICA staff, January 28, 2015.

22. *GGGI Strategic Plan 2015-2020*, p. 11.

23. Global Green Growth Institute, *Moving to Implementation: Work Program and Budget 2015-2016*, October 28, 2014, p. 13.

24. "President Park announces three-year plan for economic innovation," February 27, 2014, http://www.korea.net/NewsFocus/Policies/view?articleId-117839. Her plan aims to foster innovation, reform the public sector and social safety net, and balance

domestic demand and exports.

25. UN, "Remarks at the Climate Summit by President of the Republic of Korea," New York, September 23, 2014, http://statements.unmeetings.org/media2/4627984/rep-of-korea.pdf.

26. "Remarks by President Park Geun-hye at the World Economic Forum Annual Meeting," Geneva, January 22, 2014, http://www.korea.net/Government/Briefing-Room/Presidential-Speeches/view?articleId=117915.

27. "Hyosung Group celebrates North Jeolla R&D center," *JoongAng Daily*, November 25, 2014.

28. "Opening Remarks by President Park Geun-hye at the New Year Press Conference," Seoul, January 6, 2014, http://www.korea.net/Government/Briefing-Room/Presidential-Speeches/view?articleId=117043.

29. "Remarks by President Park Geun-hye at the Opening Ceremony of the Headquarters of the Green Climate Fund," Songdo, December 4, 2013, http://www.korea.net/Government/Briefing-Room/Presidential-Speeches/view?articleId=116702.

30. Simon Mundy, "South Korea cuts target for nuclear power," *Financial Times*, January 14, 2014.

31. Kim Se-jeong, "Higher electricity rate needed for reduction of carbon dioxide," *Korea Times*, February 26, 2014.

32. In September 2014, the South Korean government eased emission cut targets under the emissions trading scheme by 10 percent. See "Breach of promise," *Korea Times*, September 3, 2014.

33. Ipsos Global Trends 2014, http://www.ipsosglobaltrends.com/index.html.

34. "Summary of Climate Summit 2014," International Institute for Sustainable Development/Executive Office of the UN-Secretary General, September 26, 2014, http://www.iisd.ca/climate/cs/2014/html/crsvol172num18e.html.

35. Richard K. Lattanzio, "International Climate Change Financing: The Green Climate Fund (GCF)," Congressional Research Service Report, April 16, 2013.

36. Ibid.

37. Yvo de Boer, phone interview with author, February 2, 2015.

38. Ibid.

39. Urmi Goswami, "Global agreement on climate change linked to availability of financing through Green Climate Fund: Prakash Javadekar," *Economic Times,* July 13, 2014.

40. Yvo de Boer, phone interview with author, February 2, 2015.

41. Thomson Reuters Foundation online debate, "Will finance make or break new climate deal?" December 4, 2014, http://www.trust.org/spotlight/climate-finance-deal/.

42. Karl Ritter and Margie Mason, "Climate funds for coal highlight lack of UN rules," Associated Press, December 1, 2014.

43. "UN's definition of 'climate finance' comes under scrutiny," *Economic Times*, December 4, 2014.

44. Ritter and Mason, "Climate funds for coal highlight lack of UN rules."

45. Barbara Buchner, Martin Stadelmann, Jane Wilkinson, Federico Mazza, Anja Rosenberg, Dario Abramskiehn, *The Global Landscape of Climate Finance 2014*, November 2014, p. iv. This report analyzed approximately twelve thousand projects or investments in order to devise estimates of global climate finance flows. The authors also caution that their estimates of global climate finance flows should not be compared with the UNFCCC developed countries' goal of mobilizing $100 billion to assist developing countries, due to data gaps and lack of a common understanding of what constitutes climate finance.

46. Sujata Gupta, et al., "Cross-cutting Investment and Finance Issues," in *Climate Change*

2014: Mitigation of Climate Change, contribution of Working Group III to the Fifth Assessment Report of the Intergovernmental Panel on Climate Change, ed. Ottmar Edenhofer, et al. (Cambridge, UK, and New York: Cambridge University Press), p. 1210.

47. Green Climate Fund, "Private Sector Advisory Group: Initial Recommendations on the Development of the Fund's Risk Appetite," GCF/B.08/41, October 9, 2014.

48. For more information, see the following reports from the GCF's Ninth Meeting of the Board: "Private Sector Facility: Potential Approaches to Mobilizing Funding at Scale, GCF/B.09/11/Rev.01, March 6, 2015; "Private Sector Facility: Working with Local Private Entities, Including Small and Medium-Sized Enterprises," GCF/B.09/12, March 5, 2015; "Recommendations from the Private Sector Advisory Group: Private Sector Facility: Instruments to Mobilize Private Sector Resources," GCF/B.08/38, October 6, 2014.

49. For detailed information about the Private Sector Advisory Group's recommendations to the Green Climate Fund on instruments, see "Use of Other Financial Instruments," GCF/B.08/12, October 3, 2014.

50. Gupta, et al., p. 1237.

51. Buchner, et al., p. 18

52. Green Climate Fund, "Recommendations from the Private Sector Advisory Group: Private Sector Facility: Mobilizing Funds at Scale," GCF/B.08/37, October 6, 2014.

53. Yvo de Boer, phone interview with author, February 2, 2015.

54. "The Governing Instrument for the Green Climate Fund," 2011, p. 13.

55. Buchner, et al., p. vii.

56. Ibid.

57. Green Climate Fund, "Analysis of the Expected Role and Impact of the Green Climate Fund," GCF/B.09/06, February 28, 2015, p. 46.

58. For more information on the GCF's proposed adaptation performance measurement framework, see Green Climate Fund, "Further Development of the Initial Results Management Framework," GCF/B.08/07, October 6, 2014.

59. Green Climate Fund, "Initial Results Management Framework of the Fund," GCF/B.07/04, May 7, 2014, p. 6.

60. Thomson Reuters Foundation, "Will finance make or break new climate deal?"

61. Green Climate Fund, "Green Climate Fund National Designated Authority (NDA) and focal point designations," March 6, 2015, http://www.gcfund.org/fileadmin/00_customer/documents/Readiness/2014-11-14_Website_NDA_designation_list.pdf.

62. Green Climate Fund, "Frequently Asked Questions on the National Designated Authority (NDA) and Focal Point," http://www.gcfund.org/fileadmin/00_customer/documents/Readiness/2014-11-28_GCF_NDA-FP_FAQ.pdf.

63. For example, see remarks by Joyce Coffee of the Notre Dame Global Adaptation Index in Megan Rowling, "Can new global fund rescue those worst hit by climate change?" Thomson Reuters Foundation, November 19, 2014.

64. According to the GCF "Readiness Program Overview," the readiness program has an initial budget of $15 million with no more than $1 million to go toward any individual country in a calendar year, http://www.gcfund.org/fileadmin/00_customer/documents/Readiness/2014-11-28_GCF_Readiness_Overview.pdf.

65. *GGGI Strategic Plan 2015-2020*, p. 29.

66. Ibid., p. 41.

67. As of December 9, 2014, twenty-seven countries had requested readiness funds, according to "Towards an articulated vision of climate finance," statement by GCF Executive Director Hela Cheikhrouhou, Lima, Peru, December 9, 2014, http://news.gcfund.org/

wp-content/uploads/2014/12/speech_EXD_2014_12_09_lima_cop20.pdf.

68. "Latest Global Carbon Budget: Emissions Break Annual Record," September 21, 2014, http://www.globalchange.gov/news/latest-global-carbon-budget-emissions-break-annual-record.

69. Matthew Carr, "Rising German Coal Use Imperils European Emissions Deal," Bloomberg.com, June 20, 2014.

70. For example, as noted in a recent issue of *Foreign Affairs*, a 2014 study by the Center for Global Development found that "a $10 billion investment in renewable energy in Africa could bring 20 million people out of darkness, whereas an equivalent investment in natural gas could connect 90 million people to the electricity grid. In other words, prioritizing renewable energy risks leaving three out of four people in darkness who could have been given light." See Bjorn Lomborg, "Promises to Keep: Crafting Better Development Goals," *Foreign Affairs*, November/December 2014, pp. 130–138.

71. "Game⊠Changing U.S. Pledge of $3 Billion Comes Ahead of Green Climate Fund Pledging Conference," Green Climate Fund Press Release, November 15, 2014.

SOUTH KOREA AS A MIDDLE POWER:
GLOBAL AMBITIONS AND LOOMING CHALLENGES

1. Kal Holsti, "National Role Conception in the Study of Foreign Policy," *International Studies Quarterly* 14, no. 3, 1970, pp. 233–309.

2. For a recent analysis that places the United States and China at the top of the hierarchy, see Evelyn Goh, *The Struggle for Order: Hegemony, Hierarchy and Transition in Post-Cold War East Asia* (New York: Oxford University Press, 2013).

3. For instance, see G. det. Glazebrook, "The Middle Powers in the United Nations System," *International Organization* 1, no. 2, 1947, pp. 307–315; Carsten Holdbraad, *Middle Powers in International Politics* (New York: St. Martin's Press, 1984).

4. See Andrew Cooper, Richard Higgott, and Kim Nossal, *Relocating Middle Powers: Australia, Canada and the Changing World Order* (Vancouver: University of British Columbia Press, 1993).

5. Giovanni Botero, *The Reason of State* (London: Routledge & Kegan Paul, 1956), pp. 8–9, cited in Jennifer Welsh, "Canada and the World: Beyond Middle Power," in *The Oxford Handbook of Canadian Politics*, ed. John Courtney and David Smith (Oxford: Oxford University Press, 2010), p. 375.

6. Gareth Evans, "No Power? No Influence? Australia's Middle Power Diplomacy in the Asian Century," Charteris Lecture to the Australian Institute of International Affairs, New South Wales Branch, June 6, 2012, http://www.gevans.org/speeches/speech472.html.

7. For discussion, see James Manicom and Jeffrey Reeves, "Locating Middle Powers in International Relations Theory and Power Transitions," in *Middle Powers and the Rise of China*, ed. Bruce Gilley and Andrew O'Neil (Washington, DC: Georgetown University Press, 2014), pp. 23–44.

8. Republic of Korea Ministry of Foreign Affairs, "Launch of MIKTA: A Mechanism for Cooperation Between Key Regional Middle Power Countries," September 26, 2013, http://www.mofa.go.kr/webmodule/htsboard/template/read/engreadboard.jsp?boardid=302&typeID=12&tableName=TYPE_ENGLISH&seqno=312809.

9. Australian Department of Foreign Affairs and Trade, "4th MIKTA Foreign Ministers' Meeting: Joint Communique," November 26, 2014, http://foreignminister.gov.au/

releases/Pages/2014/jb_mr_141126.aspx.

10. Don Oberdorfer and Robert Carlin, *The Two Koreas: A Contemporary History*, 3rd ed. (New York: Basic Books, 2014), p. 3.

11. On this point, see Bruce Cumings, *The Korean War: A History* (New York: Random House, 2010), chap. 8.

12. The authoritative analysis of the role of ideological solidarity in alliances can be found in Stephen Walt, *The Origins of Alliances* (Ithaca: Cornell University Press, 1987), chap. 6.

13. See Julian Borger, "South Korea Considers Return of U.S. Tactical Nuclear Weapons," *Guardian*, November 23, 2010.

14. Mark Berger, *The Battle for Asia: From Decolonization to Globalization* (London: RoutledgeCurzon, 2004), p. 231.

15. Taekyoon Kim et al., "Mixed Governance and Welfare in South Korea," *Journal of Democracy* 22, no. 3, 2011, p. 122.

16. For discussion on this point, see Han Suk-hee, "South Korea Seeks to Balance Relations with China and the United States," Council on Foreign Relations, November 2012, http://www.cfr.org/south-korea/south-korea-seeks-balance-relations-china-united-states/p29447.

17. For discussion, see Gi-Wook Shin, *One Alliance, Two Lenses: U.S.-Korea Relations in a New Era* (Stanford: Stanford University Press, 2010), chaps. 6 and 7.

18. Sook-Jong Lee, "South Korea as a New Middle Power: Seeking Complex Diplomacy," EAI Asia Security Initiative Working Paper, September 2012, p. 13.

19. Young Jong Choi, "South Korea's Regional Strategy and Middle Power Activism," *Journal of East Asian Affairs* 23, no. 1, 2009, p. 53.

20. "South Korea GDP Growth Rate: 1970-2015," Trading Economics, http://www.tradingeconomics.com/south-korea/gdp-growth; and Charles Armstrong, *The Koreas*, 2nd ed. (New York: Routledge, 2013), p. 96.

21. Carl Saxer, "Capabilities and Aspirations: South Korea's Rise as a Middle Power," *Asia Europe Journal* 11, no. 2, 2013, pp. 400–401.

22. World Bank, "GDP (Constant 2005 US$): 1994," http://data.worldbank.org/indicator/NY.GDP.MKTP.KD?page=4.

23. Quoted in Sarah Teo, Bhubhinder Singh, and See Seng Tan, "South Korea's Middle Power Initiatives: Perspectives from Southeast Asia," RSIS Working Paper no. 265, November 28, 2013, p. 6.

24. For analysis of the connection between the Sunshine Policy and South Korea's leadership ambitions in Northeast Asia, see Chung-In Moon, *The Sunshine Policy: In Defense of Engagement as a Path to Peace in Korea* (Seoul: Yonsei University Press, 2012), chap. 1.

25. Heike Hermanns, "National Role Conceptions in the "Global Korea" Foreign Policy Strategy," *Korean Journal of International Studies* 11, no. 1, 2013, pp. 74–75.

26. For discussion on this point, see Jeffrey Robertson, "Middlepowerism and Continuity in South Korean Foreign Policy," *Diplomat*, May 29, 2013, http://thediplomat.com/2013/05/middlepowerism-continuity-in-south-korean-foreign-policy.

27. Kim Sung-han, "Global Governance and Middle Powers: South Korea's Role in the G20," Council on Foreign Relations, February 2013, http://www.cfr.org/south-korea/global-governance-middle-powers-south-koreas-role-g20/p30062.

28. Sook-Jong Lee, "South Korea as a New Middle Power," p. 20.

29. Hermanns, "National Role Conceptions in the 'Global Korea' Foreign Policy Strategy," p. 65.

30. See President Park Geun-hye, "An Initiative for Peaceful Unification on the Korean Peninsula," speech delivered in Dresden, Germany, March 28, 2014, http://www.koreatimes.co.kr/www/news/nation/2014/09/116_154289.html.

31. Scott Snyder, "The U.S.-ROK Alliance and the U.S. Rebalance to Asia" in *Strategic*

Asia 2014–15: U.S. Alliances and Partnerships at the Center of Global Power, ed. Ashley Tellis, Abraham Denmark, and Greg Chaffin (Seattle, WA, and Washington, DC: National Bureau of Asian Research, 2014), p. 68.

32. On the origins of the Extended Deterrence Policy Committee, see Andrew O'Neil, *Asia, the U.S. and Extended Nuclear Deterrence: Atomic Umbrellas in the Twenty-First Century* (London and New York: Routledge, 2013), pp. 66–67.

33. "Full Text of Park's Speech at U.S. Congress, May 8, 2013," Yonhap News, May 8, 2013, http://english.yonhapnews.co.kr/national/2013/05/08/4/0301000000AEN20130508 010800315F.HTML.

34. Lawrence MacDonald, "South Korea Puts Development on the Agenda for Seoul G20 Summit," *Guardian*, October 5, 2010.

35. Andrew Cooper and Ramesh Thakur, *The Group of 20* (London and New York: Routledge, 2013), p. 108.

36. Na Jeong-ju, "Korea to Share New Asia Initiative with ASEAN," *Korea Times*, October 28, 2010.

37. Young Jong Choi, "South Korea's Regional Strategy and Middle Power Activism," p. 64.

38. In 2014, the Association of Southeast Asian Nations and South Korea celebrated the twenty-fifth year of annual ASEAN-ROK dialogue, which in 2010 was formally deemed a "strategic partnership" by both sides. See ASEAN, "ASEAN-Republic of Korea Dialogue Relations," http://www.asean.org/asean/external-relations/rok/item/ asean-republic-of-korea-dialogue-relations.

39. "Remarks by President Park Geun-hye at the 2013 International Conference on Global Cooperation in the Era of Eurasia," http://www.korea.net/Government/Briefing-Room/Presidential-Speeches/view?articleId=114334. See also Jeffrey Robertson, "Seoul's Middle Power Turn in Samarkand?" *Diplomat*, July 8, 2014, http://thediplomat.com/2014/07/seouls-middle-power-turn-in-samarkand.

40. David Shim and Philipp Olbrich, "South Korea's Quest for Global Influence," *Global Asia* 7, no. 3, 2012, http://www.globalasia.org/article/south-koreas-quest-for-global-influence/.

41. Lean Alfred Santos, "South Korea Increases ODA, Pushes for 'Win-Win' Foreign Aid Policy," Devex, January 14, 2014, https://www.devex.com/news/south-korea-increases-oda-pushes-for-win-win-foreign-aid-policy-82653.

42. Arthur Andrew, *The Rise and Fall of a Middle Power: Canadian Diplomacy from King to Mulroney* (Toronto: James Lorimer & Company, 1993).

43. David Scott, "Australia as a Middle Power: Ambiguities of Role and Identity," *Seton Hall Journal of Diplomacy and International Relations*, summer/fall 2013, pp. 111–122.

44. Matthew Sussex, "The Impotence of Being Earnest? Avoiding the Pitfalls of 'Creative Middle Power Diplomacy,'" *Australian Journal of International Affairs* 65, no. 5, 2011, p. 546.

45. Geoffrey Barker, "Running the Foreign Service Under Rudd," Inside Story, August 31, 2011, http://insidestory.org.au/running-the-foreign-service-under-rudd.

46. Ralf Emmers and Sarah Teo, "Regional Security Strategies of Middle Powers in the Asia-Pacific," *International Relations of the Asia-Pacific*, forthcoming, http://irap.oxfordjournals.org/content/early/2014/12/26/irap.lcu020.short?rss=1.

47. Sook-Jong Lee, "South Korea as a New Middle Power," p. 18.

48. For analysis of South Korea's hedging strategy on the peninsula in the context of China's rise, see TongFi Kim, "South Korea's Middle Power Response to the Rise of China," in *Middle Powers and the Rise of China*, ed. Gilley and O'Neil, pp. 84–103.

49. Hedley Bull, "The New Balance of Power in Asia and the Pacific," *Foreign Affairs* 49, no. 4, 1971, pp. 669–681.

About the Authors

Colin I. Bradford is a nonresident senior fellow in the global economy and development program at the Brookings Institution. He is a specialist on global governance and the G20, and was a leading catalyst for bringing experts into consultations with officials of G20 host governments for the London, Toronto, Seoul, Cannes, Los Cabos, and Brisbane G20 summits. From 1998 to 2004 Bradford was research professor of economics and international relations and distinguished economist in residence at American University. He has served as chief economist of USAID (1994–98), head of research at the Development Centre of the Organization of Economic Cooperation and Development (OECD) in Paris (1990–94), and senior staff member in charge of the international economic outlook work of the Strategic Planning Division of the World Bank (1988–90). From 1978 to 1988, Bradford was associate director of the Yale Center for International Studies, director of the MA program in international relations, and associate professor in the practice of international economics in the Yale School of Management. He is author of numerous articles on international economic policy and development issues and editor of ten conference volumes on major international challenges. Bradford received his BA in history from Yale University and his MA and PhD in economics from Columbia University.

Toby Dalton is codirector of the nuclear policy program at the Carnegie Endowment for International Peace in Washington, DC. His research and writing focuses on cooperative nuclear security initiatives and the management of nuclear challenges in South Asia and East Asia. From 2002 to 2011, he served in several capacities at the U.S. Department of Energy's National Nuclear Security Administration, including as senior policy advisor in the Office of Nonproliferation and International Security and director of the DOE office at the U.S. Embassy in Islamabad, Pakistan. While a Luce scholar in 2001–2002, he worked as a visiting fellow at the Institute for Far Eastern Studies in Seoul, Korea. Dalton received his BA in diplomacy and world affairs from Occidental College, an MA in political science from the University of Washington, and a PhD in public policy from the George Washington University.

Brendan Howe is an international theorist from the Southwest of England, trained at Oxford University (BA/MA in modern history); the University of Kent at Canterbury (MA in international conflict analysis); and the University of Dublin, Trinity College (PhD in political science). He joined the Ewha Women's University Graduate School of International Studies in 2001 and lectures primarily on international security, organizations, politics, and negotiations. Previous posts include visiting professor at Beijing Foreign Studies University and lecturer at University Malaysia Sarawak. Howe's research leave (2007–2008) took him to Korea National Defense University and the University of Sydney. He has published extensively in the fields of Northeast Asian security, foreign policy decision-making, and humanitarian intervention. Howe is a director of the Asian Political and International Studies Association and a member of the International Institute for Security Studies.

Jill Kosch O'Donnell is a writer and lecturer who has been writing about South Korea's green growth strategy since 2010. O'Donnell currently lectures about politics and international economics for business programs at the University of Nebraska–Omaha and has also taught courses in political science and U.S. foreign policy. Previously, she worked in a variety of capacities related to international affairs in Washington, DC, including as a deputy legislative assistant for foreign policy for former U.S. Senator Chuck Hagel. O'Donnell is a graduate of Washington and Lee University in Lexington, Virginia, and holds an MA in international relations and international economics from the Johns Hopkins University's Paul H. Nitze School of Advanced International Studies. She is a member of the International Institute for Strategic Studies.

Andrew O'Neil is professor of political science and head of the School of Government and International Relations at Griffith University. From 2010 to 2014, he was director of the Griffith Asia Institute and previously associate dean for research in the Faculty of Social Sciences at Flinders University. Prior to entering academia in 2000, O'Neil worked as a Commonwealth public servant. He has taught and supervised at all levels in Australian universities and has delivered classes at Nankai, Hiroshima, and National Chengchi Universities. As part of research teams, he has won funding from the Australian Research Council (most recently for a Discovery Project on extended deterrence with Stephan Fruhling from Australia National University), and from 2009 through 2013, O'Neil was editor in chief of the *Australian Journal of International Affairs*. He is the author of two single-authored books and two coedited books, the most recent of which (with Bruce Gilley) is *Middle Powers and the Rise of China* (Georgetown University Press, 2014). O'Neil is a former member of the Australian Foreign Minister's National Consultative Committee on National Security Issues and is presently an advisory board member of the Lowy Institute's G20 Studies Centre. He is an editorial board member of the *Journal of Intelligence History,* the *Korean Journal of International Studies,* and *Security Challenges.*

Scott A. Snyder is senior fellow for Korea studies and director of the program on U.S.-Korea policy at the Council on Foreign Relations, where he had served as an adjunct fellow from 2008 to 2011. Snyder was a senior associate in the international relations program of the Asia Foundation, where he founded and directed the Center for U.S.-Korea Policy and served as the foundation's representative in Korea (2000–2004). He was also a senior associate at Pacific Forum CSIS. Snyder has worked as an Asia specialist in the research and studies program of the U.S. Institute of Peace and as acting director of the Asia Society's contemporary affairs program. He was a Pantech visiting fellow at Stanford University's Shorenstein Asia-Pacific Research Center from 2005 through 2006 and received an Abe fellowship, administered by the Social Sciences Research Council, in 1998–1999. Snyder's most recent publication (with coauthor Brad Glosserman) is *The Japan-South Korea Identity Clash: East Asian Security and the United States* (Columbia University Press, 2015).

Made in the USA
San Bernardino, CA
11 August 2015